Food Hygiene for Food Handlers

Food Hygiene for Food Handlers 2e

For more information, contact Thomson Learning, Berkshire House, 168-173 High Holborn, London, WC1V 7AA or visit us on the World Wide Web at: http://www.thomsonlearning.co.uk

British Library Cataloguing-in-Publication Data
A catalogue record for this book is available from the British Library

ISBN 1-86152-690-3

First edition published 1992 by Macmillan Press Ltd
Reprinted 1995
Second edition 1997
Reprinted 2000 by Thomson Learning

Printed in China by Central Printing Press

Food Hygiene for Food Handlers

Jill Trickett

Second Edition

THOMSON
LEARNING™

Australia • Canada • Mexico • Singapore • Spain • United Kingdom • United States

Contents

Chapter 1
Micro-organisms and Food Poisoning

Every year thousands of people suffer from food poisoning as a result of eating food that may look, taste and smell perfectly normal but is in fact contaminated with large numbers of harmful bacteria. The symptoms of food poisoning are either diarrhoea and abdominal pains *or* nausea and vomiting, although in some cases both may occur. They usually start between 1 and 36 hours after eating the contaminated food and last between 1 and 10 days. In severe cases, food poisoning can be fatal.

In the last few years, there has been an alarming increase in the number of cases of food poisoning. To reduce this number, it is essential that all people who prepare and serve food in a commercial environment or in the home should understand how food poisoning arises and how it can be prevented. One careless act causing an

An outbreak of food poisoning can ruin the reputation of a restaurant

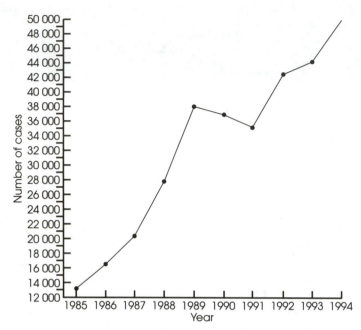

The incidence of food poisoning in England and Wales 1985–90

outbreak of food poisoning can lead to the loss of reputation or even the closure of an otherwise successful catering establishment. Fines and prison sentences can be imposed for poor hygiene standards in food premises.

Micro-organisms

Micro-organism is a general term for a small living creature that cannot be seen without using a microscope.

Micro-organisms are found everywhere: in food, water, soil and air, and on and in human and animal bodies. Many micro-organisms are completely harmless to humans and can be present in food without having any undesirable effect. Some even perform useful functions.

The micro-organisms frequently found in food fall into four main categories:

- bacteria
- yeasts
- moulds
- viruses.

Bacteria

Bacteria are the micro-organisms of greatest importance to the food hygiene specialist because the majority of cases of food poisoning are caused by them.

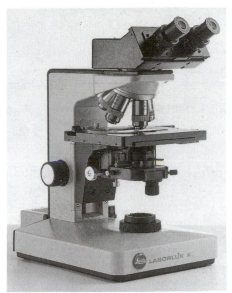

The appearance of bacteria under a microscope

Harmful bacteria
Bacteria that are capable of causing disease are called **pathogens**. With a few exceptions, small numbers of pathogenic bacteria can be swallowed without causing any ill effects, but if large numbers are present when food is eaten, they will cause food poisoning.

Spoilage bacteria
The presence of large numbers of spoilage bacteria can cause food to deteriorate in various ways:

- Milk turns sour due to the growth of bacteria that produce acids as they grow and multiply.
- Meat and fish start to smell and become slimy due to the production of waste products by the bacteria that are growing on them.

These spoilage bacteria rarely cause food poisoning. However, if food has been kept in conditions that allow the multiplication of spoilage bacteria, it is also likely that any harmful bacteria present will also have

Food which looks, smells or tastes unpleasant should not be used

had the chance to multiply. Therefore, any food that looks, smells or tastes 'off ' must not be eaten.

Useful bacteria

Not all bacteria are undesirable. For example, the production of cheese and yoghurt is dependent on the presence of large numbers of certain bacteria. In the manufacture of cheese, milk is first heated to a temperature that is high enough to kill any harmful or spoilage bacteria. Then a solution of a specific type of bacteria, known as a 'starter culture', is added. These bacteria produce the acids necessary for cheese and yoghurt production. Cheese and yoghurt therefore contain large numbers of bacteria but these are not harmful. In fact, many people claim that the bacteria used for the production of yoghurt have a beneficial effect on the human body.

Bacteria are essential for the manufacture of cheese and yoghurt

Yeasts

Yeasts do not cause food poisoning, but some types can cause food spoilage.

Spoilage yeasts
Yeasts usually spoil foods that have a high sugar content and are slightly acidic.

- Fruit juices and yoghurts that become 'fizzy' with an 'alcoholic' taste have been spoilt by yeast growth.
- Wines that become acidified have been spoilt by the growth of certain types of yeast. In the wine industry, these are called **wild yeasts**.

Useful yeasts
While some yeasts are responsible for the spoilage of wine and beer, other types are essential for the manufacture of these products. Yeast is also used in the production of bread.

Yeasts are essential for the manufacture of bread, beer and wine

Moulds

Harmful moulds
Moulds do not cause food poisoning with the typical symptoms of sudden vomiting and diarrhoea but some are capable of causing illness due to the production of **mycotoxins** (poisonous substances). Mould growth and mycotoxin production are a particular problem in tropical countries where grain and nuts are stored in damp conditions at high temperatures. In these countries, there is a high incidence of liver

disease in people who consume mouldy grain and nuts, and hence mycotoxins, over a long period of time. It is not acceptable practice to scrape off the mould on the surface of the food and to use the food underneath because the mould penetrates further into the food. Since many moulds are capable of producing mycotoxins it should be assumed that all mouldy food is unfit to eat.

Spoilage moulds
Many foods are spoilt by mould growth on the surface. A black, blue-green or white hairy growth is a familiar sight on bread, cheese, jams, vegetables and fruits (especially if the skin is damaged).

The growth of mould on the surface of food is a familiar sight

Useful moulds
Certain types of mould that are known to be harmless are injected into cheese during its manufacture to produce the familiar blue cheeses.

Viruses

Viruses are even smaller than bacteria. They cannot live independently and only multiply in living tissue. Some viruses cause vomiting and diarrhoea. They can be transferred in food from the person who prepares the food to the person who eats it, although the viruses do not actually multiply in the food.

Oysters, cockles and mussels are a frequent cause of viral food poisoning. They are known as 'filter feeders' and when harvested from sewage-polluted water they have a high concentration of bacteria and viruses in their flesh. As viruses are easily destroyed by heat, shellfish and other foods contaminated with viruses can be made safe to eat by thorough cooking.

Not as much is known about viral food poisoning as bacterial food poisoning, but it seems likely that many of the 'tummy bugs' that do not appear to be caused by bacteria are in fact caused by viruses.

Summary of the effect of micro-organisms on food

Micro-organism	Effect
Bacteria	• Contamination of food leading to food poisoning. • Spoilage of certain foods, particularly moist, protein foods, e.g., milk and meat. • Production of some foods, e.g., cheese and yoghurt.
Yeasts	• Spoilage of high-sugar, acid foods, e.g., fruit juices, yoghurt and wine. • Production of beer, wine and bread.
Moulds	• Production of mycotoxins. • Blue-green/white/black discolouration of food, particularly dry or acid foods, e.g., bread and citrus fruits. • Production of blue cheeses.
Viruses	• Contamination of food leading to food poisoning.

Other causes of poisoning associated with food

Sickness and more severe illness can also be caused by eating poisonous plants or by ingesting chemicals. However, both these causes of poisoning are much less common than bacterial food poisoning.

Fungi

Many fungi that look similar to mushrooms are poisonous, so anyone collecting fungi from the fields to eat must be certain that they are able to distinguish the edible ones from the poisonous ones. For example,

Edible or poisonous fungi?

consumption of the death cap fungus, as its name suggests, usually has fatal consequences.

Berries

Children are often tempted to eat berries from trees, but many of these are poisonous. Deadly nightshade and the seeds from the laburnum tree cause serious illness.

Red kidney beans

Undercooked red kidney beans can cause severe vomiting, even if only a few beans are eaten. This is due to a naturally occurring poison which can only be destroyed by *boiling* the beans for at least 10 minutes. Dishes containing red kidney beans must not be cooked in a slow-cook oven unless the beans have been boiled first, because slow-cook ovens do not bring the temperature of the food up to boiling point. Canned red kidney beans are quite safe to eat without further cooking.

Chemicals

A few cases of food poisoning are caused by the accidental consumption of chemicals, such as cleaning agents, often because they have been stored in unmarked or incorrectly labelled bottles, e.g., lemonade bottles. Any bottle containing poisonous chemicals must be *clearly marked* with its contents.

Empty food and drink containers must not be used to store chemicals

Metals

Traces of poisonous metals can get into food from cooking utensils, particularly when they are used with acid foods. Galvanised iron containers can cause zinc poisoning while chipped enamel vessels can cause antimony poisoning. Copper saucepans should not be used for cooking or storing very acid foods such as chutney and pickles.

Canned foods may also cause metal poisoning. When a can of food is opened any remaining food that is not required immediately should be emptied into a non-metallic container. Any imperfection in the lacquer coating inside the can allows the food to absorb iron and tin, both of which are poisonous. Acid foods (e.g., citrus fruits and tomato products) and the presence of oxygen (an open can) greatly increase the rate of metal absorption.

Never keep food in a can after it has been opened

Chapter 2

Bacterial Growth

Danger Zone Temps.
40° — 140°

Bacteria are very small and consist of only one cell. Thousands of bacterial cells would fit on a pin head. They are usually rod shaped or spherical, although a few are comma shaped or spiral.

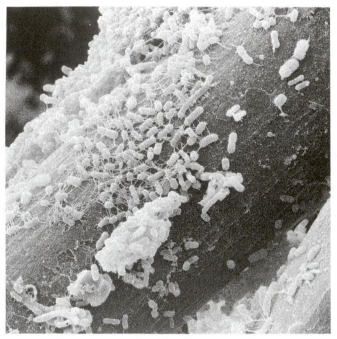

Individual bacteria can only be seen through a microscope. These are on a kitchen scourer and are magnified 2000 times

Reproduction

Bacteria reproduce very simply by growing to a certain size and then splitting into two individual cells, which then both increase in size and again split into two cells. This process is known as **binary fission**. In ideal conditions, binary fission can take place approximately every 20

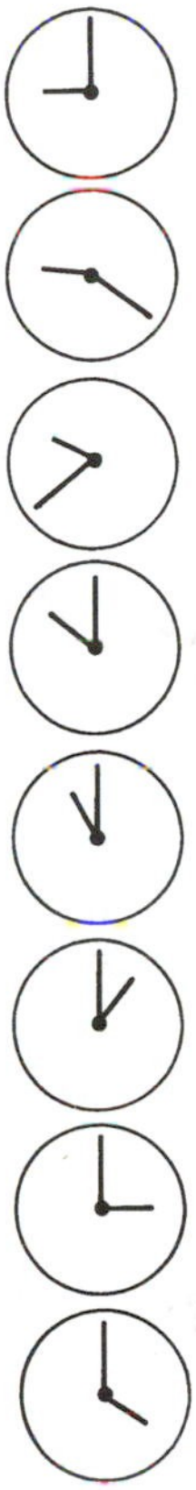

Time		Number of bacterial cells	Time passed
9.00		1	0
9.20		2	20 minutes
9.40		4	40 minutes
10.00		8	1 hour
11.00		64	2 hours
13.00		4096	4 hours
15.00		262 144	6 hours
16.00		2 097 152	7 hours

In ideal conditions, bacteria double their numbers every 20 minutes

minutes. Hence, this method of reproduction results in a very rapid increase in the total number of bacterial cells.

Conditions necessary for bacterial growth

Bacteria have four requirements for growth and multiplication:

- warmth
- food
- moisture
- time.

Warmth

Most bacteria need warm temperatures to multiply. The bacteria that cause food poisoning will grow and multiply most rapidly at 37°C, which is the normal temperature of the human body. However, they will multiply at any temperature between 8°C and 63°C, although their rate of reproduction is much slower at the lower and higher end of this temperature range than at 37°C. The temperature range of 8°C to 63°C is known as the **danger zone**.

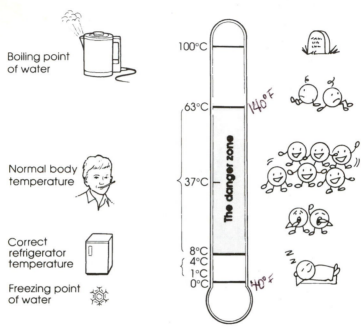

Boiling point of water

Normal body temperature

Correct refrigerator temperature

Freezing point of water

100°C

63°C

37°C

8°C
4°C
1°C
0°C

140°F

The danger zone

40°F

The effect of temperature on bacterial growth

Food

Like all living things, bacteria need a source of energy and raw materials to grow. Not all the food we eat will support bacterial growth. Food containing high concentrations of sugar, salt and acid will not normally support the multiplication of bacteria, e.g., jams, syrups, salted meats and pickles.

The foods that will support bacterial growth, and are therefore most likely to cause food poisoning, are called **high-risk foods**. They contain protein and moisture, and are usually eaten without further cooking.

High-risk foods

The following foods will support bacterial multiplication if kept at temperatures within the danger zone:

- cooked meat and poultry, meat pies, pâté, soups, stocks, gravy and gelatin

- milk, cream, eggs, soft cheeses and foods containing them as ingredients, e.g., quiches, trifles and cream cakes
- shellfish and other seafoods
- cooked rice.

High-risk foods must be stored in a refrigerator

Raw meat

Raw meat encourages bacterial multiplication and must be kept refrigerated. It is not included in the list of high-risk foods because it is normally cooked before being eaten. The cooking process destroys most of the bacteria present, so meat that has been thoroughly cooked is not likely to be a cause of food poisoning. However, raw meat is one of the most frequent causes of contamination of high-risk foods (see p. 18).

Moisture

Bacteria need water for growth and multiplication. All high-risk foods contain sufficient water for bacterial growth. However, bacteria can

Reconstituted powders must be stored in a refrigerator

also survive in dry foods such as milk powder, cornflour, custard powder and egg powder. They do not grow and reproduce but remain dormant (alive but inactive). When moisture is added to the dry foods, the dormant bacteria can grow and multiply again.

Time

If bacteria are given a suitable temperature, food and moisture, they simply need time to multiply. In a relatively short time, a few pathogenic bacteria (which are often present in food) will multiply to a sufficiently large number to cause food poisoning when the food is eaten.

If food is eaten soon after it is cooked or prepared, the risk of food poisoning is substantially reduced

How many bacteria must be present to cause food poisoning?

With most types of bacterial food poisoning, one million or more bacteria must be present in the food before a healthy adult will have any symptoms of food poisoning, although people do vary in their susceptibility. A young child or an elderly or sick person is likely to be affected by the presence of fewer bacteria. Special care must therefore be taken when preparing food for these people.

It is not unusual for food to be contaminated with several hundred food poisoning bacteria. If the food is a high-risk food and is kept at a warm temperature, these bacteria could multiply to over one million in three or four hours.

Destruction of bacteria by heat

Bacteria that cause food poisoning will not multiply at temperatures above 63°C and as the temperature increases above this, they will gradually be destroyed. The higher the temperature, the shorter the time necessary for their destruction. Most are killed by normal cooking methods but a few types are able to survive in a resistant form known as a **spore** (see below).

Effect of storage at low temperatures on bacteria

Although bacteria are not destroyed at low temperatures, most food poisoning bacteria will not multiply below 8°C but will remain dormant in the food. *Listeria* bacteria (see p. 94) are an exception in this respect because they can grow slowly at the temperature of a refrigerator (1°C–4°C).

Some spoilage bacteria are able to grow slowly in a refrigerator, but the rate of multiplication, and hence the rate of spoilage, will be much slower than at room temperature (20°C). For example, milk turns sour in one to two days at room temperature but will last four to five days in a refrigerator. Raw fish will smell 'off' in less than a day at room temperature but will last approximately two days in a refrigerator. The storage life of raw fish is short because it comes from a cold environment (the sea) and carries many spoilage bacteria that are able to grow at low temperatures.

Bacteria can remain dormant for long periods of time in frozen food, but when the food is thawed and warmed up, they start to multiply again.

Spores

Most bacteria will not survive for long at high temperatures or in unsuitable environmental conditions. However, a few types of food poisoning bacteria are able to protect themselves when conditions are

Some types of bacteria can survive cooking processes by forming spores

not suitable for growth by forming a spore. Spores are protective casings that enable bacteria to survive cooking processes. The bacteria do not grow and multiply in the spore form, but if the temperature of the cooked food is reduced, so that it is once more in the danger zone (8°C–63°C), they start to multiply again.

Bacteria in the spore form can survive for years if insufficient moisture is present. They return to active growth and multiplication when moisture is again present. Bacteria are also more resistant to chemicals in the spore form and hence may survive disinfection.

Toxins

Some food poisoning bacteria, but not all, produce a poisonous substance, known as a **toxin**, while they are growing and multiplying in food. As the toxin is often more resistant to heat than the bacterial cell, it is possible for the food to be poisonous even if no live bacteria are present.

Case History

A group of 12 people became ill with severe vomiting two hours after eating a meal from a take-away restaurant one Friday night in summer. The only food that they had all eaten was fried rice. Investigations revealed that, due to the heavy demand for meals on Friday nights, the chef had boiled the rice the day before and stored it in the kitchen overnight, since there was insufficient space in the refrigerator. The next evening, the rice had been reheated by flash frying – a quick heating in hot fat.

On investigation, samples of rice from the restaurant were found to contain large numbers of bacteria called *Bacillus cereus*. *Bacillus cereus* forms spores that survive the initial boiling of the rice, and so the bacteria are able to multiply again when the rice cools down to a temperature within the danger zone. *Bacillus cereus* also produces a toxin that survives the flash frying.

1. The rice is boiled the evening before it is required.

2. The rice is stored at room temperature overnight.

3. The rice is reheated quickly. The toxin produced by the bacteria overnight is not destroyed.

4. The people who had eaten the rice became ill very suddenly.

Fault

Cooked rice, which is a high-risk food, was kept for 24 hours at a temperature within the danger zone.

Chapter 3
Food Contamination

To prevent food poisoning, it is essential not to contaminate high-risk foods with bacteria.

Sources of contamination

The main sources of contamination in a kitchen are:

- raw meat and poultry
- food handlers
- animals, rodents, birds and insects
- dust and refuse.

Raw meat and poultry

The intestines of animals and poultry frequently carry bacteria that cause food poisoning. For example, approximately 70% of chickens carry bacteria called *Salmonella*. In the slaughter house the surface of the raw meat becomes contaminated with bacteria from the animal's intestine. Therefore, it is safer to assume that raw meat and poultry, as well as the juices that come from them, are contaminated with food poisoning bacteria.

Ways to prevent contamination by raw meat and poultry

- Transport raw meat in refrigerated vehicles used only for that purpose.
- Always store cooked meat above raw meat in a refrigerator, or if possible store them in different refrigerators.
- Allocate separate areas for preparing raw meat and high-risk foods.
- Use different chopping boards and utensils for the preparation of raw meat and high-risk foods (see colour coding p. 23).
- Always wash your hands after preparing raw meat.

Always keep raw meat and poultry well separated from cooked food

Food handlers

The bacteria that cause food poisoning may be present in and on the human body. Bacteria called *Staphylococcus aureus* are found on the hands, under the fingernails and in the nose, throat and mouth of many people. When present in these areas of the body, these bacteria do not cause any harm and so their presence goes unnoticed. However, they do cause illness when they, or the toxins they produce, get into the intestinal tract in large numbers.

Open cuts and wounds are a source of *Staphylococcus aureus* and so should always be adequately covered with a waterproof plaster to prevent the contamination of food. Septic cuts and boils contain millions of bacteria and so anyone with a septic cut or boil on the hands or face should not handle high-risk foods.

A person harbouring food poisoning bacteria in the intestinal tract is called a **carrier** – either a **convalescent carrier** or a **healthy carrier**. A convalescent carrier is someone who has recently recovered from food poisoning but is still harbouring pathogenic bacteria in his/her intestines. A healthy carrier is someone who has had no symptoms of food poisoning but is nevertheless harbouring pathogenic bacteria in his/her intestines. Pathogenic bacteria will be passed in the faeces of both convalescent and healthy carriers and are likely to be transferred to the carrier's hands during visits to the toilet.

Ways to prevent contamination by food handlers

- Do not sneeze or cough over food.
- Where possible, use serving tongs for handling cooked food.
- Do not handle high-risk foods when suffering from septic cuts or boils.
- Always wash your hands after visiting the toilet.
- Do not handle high-risk foods while suffering from or recovering from food poisoning.

Use serving tongs when handling high-risk foods

Animals, rodents, birds and insects

Pets, rodents, cockroaches and insects frequently carry food poisoning bacteria in their intestinal tracts, as well as on their bodies and feet. For this reason, food that has been partly eaten or licked by animals or insects must be discarded, and any food preparation surfaces where they have walked must be cleaned and disinfected.

Bird droppings and feathers are heavily contaminated with food poisoning bacteria and so every effort must be made to keep birds out of the kitchen.

Flies spread food poisoning bacteria to food because they vomit and defecate on it while they are feeding.

Ways to prevent contamination by animals, rodents, birds and insects

- Keep the doors of industrial kitchens shut and the windows covered with mesh.
- Make regular checks to ensure that rodents and cockroaches are not present (see p. 76).
- Install electronic fly killers in industrial kitchens.
- Do not allow pets in food preparation rooms.

Keep pets out of the kitchen

Dust and refuse

Soil and dust contain spores of food poisoning bacteria called *Clostridium perfringens*. It is therefore important that kitchens are cleaned regularly and kept relatively free of dust. Soil and dirt must be removed from fresh vegetables before they come into contact with other foods.

Waste food in refuse bins in a warm kitchen provides ideal conditions for bacteria to live and to reproduce.

Ways to prevent contamination by dust and refuse

- Clean raw vegetables in a separate preparation area from high-risk foods.
- Cover food and store it away when dusting and sweeping the food preparation area.
- Empty refuse bins frequently and never allow them to overflow.

Store food away before dusting or sweeping food preparation areas

Cross-contamination

Raw meat, food handlers, animals and dust are all sources of bacteria and bacteria are often transferred from them to high-risk foods by a process known as **cross-contamination**.

Cross-contamination is the transfer of bacteria from a contaminated source to an uncontaminated food via a non-food 'vehicle'. The 'vehicle' involved is usually one of the following:

- hands of a food handler
- utensils, chopping boards, work surfaces, cloths or other equipment
- droplets of moisture from sneezing or coughing
- drops of liquid from a contaminated food.

Even if cross-contamination to a high-risk food does occur, the high-risk food does not always become poisonous immediately. But, if that food is left at a warm temperature for several hours, the bacteria transferred to it will multiply rapidly and the food will cause food poisoning when it is eaten.

Cross-contamination of food during its preparation can cause food poisoning. In this illustration the same knife is used for jointing raw chicken and slicing cooked ham. Two hundred bacteria are transferred to the cooked ham which is then left in a warm kitchen, allowing bacteria to multiply rapidly.

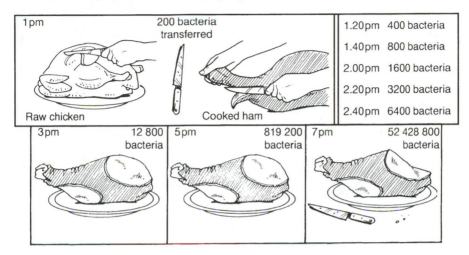

1pm	200 bacteria transferred	1.20pm 400 bacteria
		1.40pm 800 bacteria
		2.00pm 1600 bacteria
		2.20pm 3200 bacteria
Raw chicken	Cooked ham	2.40pm 6400 bacteria
3pm 12 800 bacteria	5pm 819 200 bacteria	7pm 52 428 800 bacteria

Colour coding of equipment

Equipment such as chopping boards and knives should be used in the preparation of only one type of food to avoid cross-contamination between raw and cooked foods. A colour coding system (in which a small coloured tag is fixed to the equipment) can be used to identify which equipment can be used for which type of food.

Colour code	Equipment to be used only for:
Red	Raw meat and poultry
Green	Fruits and vegetables
Blue	Raw fish
Brown	Cooked meats
White	Dairy products

Case History

Several incidents of food poisoning were reported in a West London suburb. A total of 19 people were traced who had become ill with diarrhoea and vomiting approximately 16 hours after eating chicken curry at one particular restaurant.

On investigation, it was found that frozen chickens had been delivered to the premises in plastic containers and had been left in them to defrost. After spit roasting, the chickens had been put back in the same plastic containers until the chef had time to remove the flesh. The meat had then been added to a warm curry sauce and served to customers.

1. Frozen chickens are delivered to the restaurant in plastic containers. They are left in them to defrost.

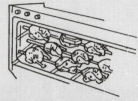

2. The chickens are spit roasted.

3. The chickens are put back in the same plastic containers to cool.

4. A chef removes the meat from the carcasses.

5. The meat is stirred into warm curry sauce and served to customers.

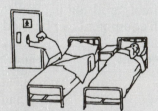

6. The customers suffer from diarrhoea and vomiting.

Faults

1. The freshly cooked chicken was cross-contaminated when it was put back into the plastic containers that had held the raw chicken.
2. Bacteria had chance to multiply before the meat was removed from the bone.
3. When the chicken meat was heated up in the warm sauce, the temperature reached was not high enough to destroy the bacteria present.

Chapter 4
Personal Hygiene for Food Handlers

Bacteria live in and on the human body and people frequently carry food poisoning bacteria on their skin, in their noses or in their intestinal tract. Therefore, it is very important that food handlers keep themselves clean while working in the kitchen and avoid unhygienic habits that could spread bacteria to the food they are preparing.

Hand-washing

Wash your hands frequently throughout the working day

The hands are in direct contact with food during its preparation and are frequently responsible for transferring bacteria to high-risk foods. To avoid cross-contaminating foods, food handlers should wash their hands frequently throughout the working day, particularly at the following times:

- after using the toilet
- on entering the kitchen and before touching any food or equipment
- after handling raw meat, poultry, vegetables and eggs
- after handling waste food or refuse
- after coughing into the hands or using a handkerchief
- after smoking or eating
- after combing the hair
- after carrying out any cleaning task.

Hands must be washed with hot water and liquid soap in basins specifically provided for this purpose (never at sinks allocated for food preparation). Nails must be kept short, as bacteria tend to collect under them, and they should be scrubbed with a clean, nylon-bristled nailbrush each time the hands are washed. Nail varnish should not be used.

Hands must be thoroughly dried by using disposable paper towels, a hot air dryer or a continuous roller towel.

Protective clothing

As ordinary clothing is frequently contaminated with dust and hair, all food handlers should wear clean, washable, light-coloured overalls and aprons to protect the food that they are preparing from contamination. Lockers should be provided for coats and outdoor clothing, which must not be brought into the food preparation area.

Hair should be kept clean and covered with a net or hat to prevent loose hairs and dandruff falling into food. Hair combing and adjustments to hats should be done in the cloakroom before putting on clean overalls.

Jewellery

Food handlers should not wear any jewellery other than plain wedding rings while working in the kitchen. The skin under jewellery tends to harbour bacteria, particularly if it is not thoroughly dried after washing. There is also a danger that stones and small parts of rings, ear-rings and necklaces may drop into food.

Food handlers must wear clean overalls and hats

Smoking

It is illegal to smoke in a commercial kitchen or while handling open food – anyone found doing so can be fined. The main reason for this is that people touch their lips while smoking and may transfer harmful bacteria on to their hands and so to food.

It is against the law to smoke while preparing food

Nose and mouth

Food poisoning bacteria called *Staphylococcus aureus* are frequently carried in the nose and throat of healthy individuals. Care must therefore be taken not to cough or sneeze over food or working surfaces because the droplets of moisture expelled may carry large numbers of these bacteria. For this reason, a food handler with a heavy cold should not handle high-risk foods. While working in the kitchen, it is better to use disposable tissues, which are destroyed after one use, rather than ordinary handkerchiefs, which will harbour bacteria and become a source of infection themselves.

Other habits that are unacceptable in a food room are: nailbiting, spitting, eating sweets and chewing gum, tasting food with a finger or an unwashed spoon, licking the fingers to separate sheets of wrapping paper, or blowing on cutlery or glasses before polishing them.

Cuts, boils and septic spots

Any cut or sore must be covered with a coloured waterproof dressing immediately, otherwise it will quickly become infected. A blue or other dark-coloured plaster should be used in preference to a skin-coloured one, as it will be seen more easily if it accidentally falls into food. Food that has come into contact with the plaster must not be used.

Anyone suffering from septic cuts, boils, styes and whitlows should not handle open food because the risk of infecting the food is too great.

Reporting illness

If a food handler feels unwell he/she should report it to his/her supervisor or manager, particularly if the symptoms include vomiting or diarrhoea. This also applies to food handlers who have just returned from abroad and have suffered from vomiting or diarrhoea while there, even if the symptoms are no longer present. Food handlers should also inform their supervisor if someone living in the same house as them is suffering from food poisoning, even if the food handler himself has no symptoms.

Report all skin, throat and bowel problems to your supervisor. Do not spread infection by handling food.

The duty of the supervisor is to contact an environmental health officer who will carry out investigations if necessary. A food handler who is suffering from vomiting and diarrhoea will not be allowed to work with food for 48 hours after the symptoms have ceased. Compensation for loss of earnings will be paid by the local authority.

Similarly, food handlers with skin or throat infections or discharges from the eyes or ears will be excluded from work until medical clearance is given.

Case History

A coach party of people on their way to the seaside were provided with ham sandwiches prepared at a public house. Between three and four hours after eating the sandwiches, the members of the party who had eaten them suffered from severe vomiting. Some were sufficiently ill to need hospital treatment.

Investigations at the public house revealed that the chef who had prepared the sandwiches had a heavy cold and had used the same handkerchief repeatedly to blow her nose. She had sliced the ham the day before preparing the sandwiches and left it overnight in a refrigerator that was found to be running at a temperature of 17°C. Early the next morning, the sandwiches were prepared and put on the coach in uninsulated containers, where they were left for three hours before being eaten. It was a very

1. The chef slices the ham while repeatedly blowing her nose.

2. The slices of ham are left overnight in a refrigerator running at 17°C.

3. The sandwiches are put on the coach in uninsulated containers and are eaten approximately three hours later.

4. The members of the party who had eaten the sandwiches became ill with severe vomiting.

warm day and the temperature inside the coach was high. The chef's nasal secretions were found to contain enormous numbers of *Staphylococcus aureus* and her hands were also covered with the bacteria.

Faults

1. The chef should not have prepared high-risk foods when suffering from a heavy cold.
2. When working in the kitchen, disposable paper handkerchiefs should be used and destroyed after a single use. Hands should be washed after blowing the nose.
3. The temperature of the refrigerator was too high. It should be between 1°C and 4°C.
4. The sandwiches should have been stored in a cool box on the long coach journey.

Chapter 5

Correct Food Handling Procedures

Correct temperature control of food is the single most important consideration when preparing food if food poisoning is to be avoided. Care taken to prevent cross-contamination during food preparation will significantly reduce the numbers of food poisoning bacteria found on food. However, as a few bacteria are still likely to be present, every effort must be made to keep the temperature of high-risk foods out of the danger zone (8°C–63°C) so that bacterial multiplication cannot take place.

The majority of cases of food poisoning that occur each year are caused by keeping food at room temperature, rather than storing it under refrigeration, or by cooking it in such a way that it spends most of the cooking period at a temperature within the danger zone (8°C–63°C).

In the summer, the temperature in a badly ventilated kitchen can reach 37°C, which is the temperature at which food poisoning bacteria grow most rapidly. At any time of year, the temperature in a busy kitchen, with many cooking appliances in use, will be higher than the average room temperature of 20°C.

Two basic rules with regard to the temperature control of food

1. Keep food hot (above 63°C). 145°

    OR

2. Keep food cold (below 8°C). 48°

To ensure that these aims are achieved when preparing food, the following precautions must be taken:

- Frozen meat must be completely thawed before cooking.
- Food must be cooked thoroughly and served immediately, or cooled rapidly and refrigerated until it is ready to be served or reheated.
- If food has to be reheated, it should be thoroughly reheated so that the temperature in the centre of the food is above 70°C. It should never be reheated more than once.

Keep food hot (above 63°C) or cold (below 8°C) until it is ready to be served

Thawing food

Many foods can be taken from the freezer and cooked without thawing, but poultry, joints of meat and large volumes of food must be completely thawed before cooking. *Salmonella* food poisoning has often been caused because chickens and turkeys have not been thoroughly defrosted before cooking. During cooking, heat travels from the outside to the centre of food. If ice is present in the centre of a carcass, a great deal of heat will be needed to melt the ice with the result that the temperature reached in the centre of the bird during the cooking period will not be high enough to kill bacteria. Instead, it will probably reach a temperature within the danger zone (8°C–63°C), which will allow any bacteria present to multiply.

A great deal of heat is needed to melt ice in the centre of a large volume of food

Some catering establishments use special thawing cabinets for thawing meat. These cabinets operate by maintaining a constant cool temperature between 10°C and 15°C. The use of one of these cabinets for raw meat only also ensures that cross-contamination from the raw meat to other foods in the kitchen does not take place.

If a thawing cabinet is not available, it is best to thaw small joints of meat and chickens in a refrigerator. As food poisoning bacteria are almost always present on raw meat, it is very important to ensure that liquid from the thawing meat does not come into contact with any other food in the refrigerator. Ideally, a separate refrigerator should be used for raw meat, but if only one is available, the raw meat should be placed in a container that is deep enough to hold any liquid lost from the meat during thawing. The container must then be placed on the bottom shelf of the refrigerator to prevent cross-contamination to cooked foods, which should always be placed on the top shelves above the raw meat. A 1.5 kg (3.3 lb) chicken takes approximately 24 hours to thaw in a refrigerator, so chickens of this size should be removed from the freezer one day before they are needed for cooking.

Turkeys and large joints of meat are probably best thawed in a cool area of the kitchen, if no thawing cabinet is available. Thawing in a refrigerator can take too long (up to four days), so it is better to try to

"Christmas Greetings"

Allow sufficient time for poultry to thaw completely before cooking

speed up the process by leaving the meat at a temperature of approximately 15°C, at which bacterial growth is relatively slow. Thawing meat should not be placed near a heat source, such as a cooker or a radiator, nor should it be immersed in warm water to defrost it, because this would allow bacteria on the surface to grow rapidly while the centre is defrosting. Poultry is properly defrosted when the legs move freely and there are no ice crystals in the flesh or in the central cavity.

When food has been thawed, it should be kept in a refrigerator and cooked within 24 hours. It must never be refrozen, unless it has been cooked thoroughly after thawing.

Cooking food

Food is a poor conductor of heat. The larger the volume of food, the longer it will take for heat to reach the centre during cooking. For this reason, the maximum size of a joint of meat should be 3 kg (6.6 lb), so that sufficient heat to kill bacteria reaches the centre during the cooking period. An exception to this rule can be made for a solid joint of meat with no bone. Most bacterial contamination is on the surface of meat, so it is safe to cook and to serve rare beef, even though the temperature reached in the centre during cooking may not have been high enough to kill bacteria – the temperature on the surface will have been high enough to destroy any food poisoning bacteria present.

Rolled joints and minced meat dishes need to be treated differently from solid joints, as bacteria originally present on the surface of the meat are rolled into the centre or distributed throughout the meat. In both these cases, it is essential that the temperature in the centre of the food reaches at least 70°C for a minimum of two minutes. A probe

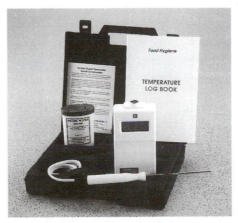

Use a probe thermometer to measure the temperature in the centre of a large volume of food

thermometer should be used to ensure that this temperature is reached.

Similarly, it is not recommended to cook poultry with the cavity of the bird filled with stuffing. The stuffing slows down heat penetration so that, by the time the outside is cooked, the temperature in the centre of the bird may not be high enough to destroy food poisoning bacteria. It is safer to cook the stuffing separately.

Food should be eaten as soon as possible after cooking. If it has to be kept hot for a short time prior to serving, it must be kept at a temperature above 63°C. Hot plates can be used for this purpose, but they are only suitable for keeping hot food hot and must never be used to heat up cold food (see p. 51).

Cooling food

If food is to be served cold, it must be cooled as rapidly as possible after cooking. However, food that has just been cooked should not be transferred straight from the oven to the refrigerator, as this would increase the temperature of the refrigerator above the maximum recommended temperature of 4°C. (A higher temperature in the refrigerator would allow the multiplication of any bacteria present in other foods being stored there and would also encourage condensation and consequently cross-contamination from one food to another.) When food is removed from the oven, it should be covered loosely with aluminium foil or greaseproof paper and placed in a chiller (see p. 46) or in the coldest

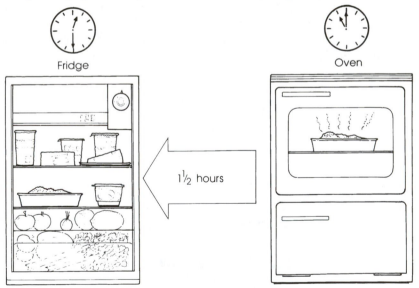

Fridge

Oven

1½ hours

Food should be cooled to 15°C or less within 1½ hours of cooking and then stored in a refrigerator

area in the kitchen, but this must not be the same area of the kitchen that is used for defrosting raw meat. If it is possible to divide the cooked food into smaller portions, it will cool more quickly. Casseroles or saucepans of hot food can be placed in a sink of ice or cold water and stirred occasionally with a clean utensil to speed up the cooling process. Food should be put in the refrigerator within 11/2 hours of cooking and must be stored there until just before serving.

Reheating food

Reheating either meat dishes or rice dishes is not good practice, since both meat and rice are usually contaminated with the types of food poisoning bacteria that form spores. The initial cooking period does not destroy spores and when the food is cooled down the spores germinate and bacteria start to multiply as the temperature passes through the danger zone (8°C–63°C). If food is refrigerated, the bacteria become dormant, but when the food is reheated, they start to multiply again as the temperature passes through the danger zone. A high-risk food should therefore never be reheated more than once, since each time it

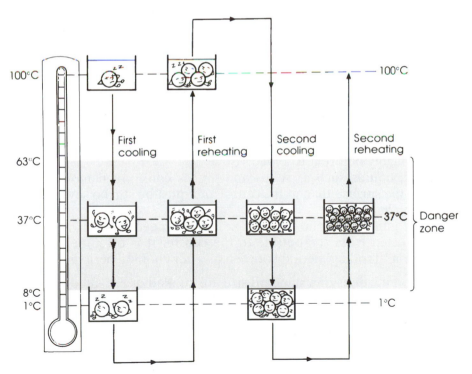

A high-risk food should never be reheated more than once

is reheated there are two opportunities for bacteria to multiply, once during the cooling process and once during the heating process. In schools and hospitals, the usual policy is not to reheat foods at all, since children and sick people are particularly susceptible to food poisoning.

For the same reason, meat dishes should not be part-cooked one day with the intention of finishing the cooking process the next day. Bacteria in the centre of the product will not be destroyed during partial cooking and will multiply while the food is cooling on the first day and again when it is being reheated the next day.

Microwave ovens

Any catering establishment that uses a microwave oven regularly for cooking or reheating food must use a commercial microwave oven. Domestic microwave ovens have a life expectancy of only 2000 hours and they usually have an output between 500 and 700 watts. Commercial microwave ovens are designed to last for many more hours of use and have an output between 700 and 1600 watts so that food can be reheated quickly.

To prevent food poisoning when microwave cooking, the same principles must be applied as in conventional cooking.

1. Always defrost food completely before starting a cooking cycle.
2. Cook food thoroughly.
3. Never reheat food more than once.

It is important to remember that different foods respond in different ways to microwave cooking.

- Irregular shapes such as chicken joints do not cook evenly. It is important to check that all areas of the chicken have been cooked thoroughly before it is served.
- Thick liquids such as soups and sauces cook much more quickly near the surface than at the centre and must be stirred several times during heating.
- Meat joints and solid foods, e.g., lasagne, need time for heat to be conducted from the outside to the centre. It is often necessary to allow a 'standing' period between or after cooking periods.

If food portions of a standard size are cooked or reheated regularly, it is useful to display a chart giving the length of time required, the power setting and the standing time necessary for adequate cooking.

Liquids sometimes 'erupt' when they are taken from the microwave oven and have been known to cause serious burns. Microwave cooking does not heat foods evenly and parts of the food can become superheated. These 'hot spots' can form in any liquid but are more likely to occur in viscous liquids such as gravy and custard.

To avoid accidents when heating liquids, the following guidelines should be followed:

- Stir before placing in the microwave oven. This will incorporate bubbles in the liquid which help to prevent the formation of 'hot spots'.
- Use a container which is wider at the top than at the base.
- Stir half-way through the cooking period.
- Let the liquid stand in the microwave oven for a short time after heating.

Microwave ovens should be cleaned regularly, particularly around the door seal, because the presence of dirt and grease may stop the door closing correctly. They should be checked every year to ensure there is no leakage of microwaves. Local environmental health departments frequently provide a testing service.

Case History

A serious outbreak of food poisoning occurred in a hospital. A total of 180 patients complained of severe diarrhoea and abdominal pains between 12 and 16 hours after eating a meal of savoury mince, potatoes and peas.

On investigation, it was found that the minced meat had been cooked the day before serving and had been covered and left to cool overnight in the kitchen, since there was no room in the refrigerator. The next day the meat was reheated quickly and served. A sample of the meal was analysed and found to contain large numbers of the bacteria called *Clostridium perfringens*. *Clostridium perfringens* forms spores that enable the bacteria to survive the initial cooking period, allowing them to multiply when the mince is cooling down and the temperature is in the danger zone.

1. The minced meat is cooked the day before it is required.

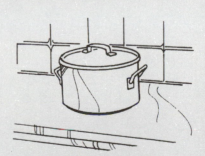

2. It is covered and left to cool in the kitchen because there is no space in the refrigerator.

3. The meat is heated up quickly and served.

Faults

1. The minced meat was cooled too slowly after cooking and was not put in a refrigerator within $1\frac{1}{2}$ hours.
2. The reheating process was inadequate.

Chapter 6
Food Storage

Food must be stored under the right conditions so that it is safe to eat. These conditions depend on the nature of the food and the length of time for which it is to be stored.

Heat treatment of foods

Some foods are heat treated before they are sold to the public to reduce the risk of food poisoning. The temperature and the length of time for which the food is heated determine the number and type of micro-organisms that will be killed. In general, spoilage micro-organisms can withstand higher temperatures for longer periods than pathogenic organisms.

The two main methods of heat treatment applied to foods are **sterilisation** and **pasteurisation**. Sterilisation is a heat process that is designed to destroy all micro-organisms and their spores. Pasteurisation is a milder heat process that is designed to reduce the number of spoilage micro-organisms and destroy all the pathogenic ones. Ultra-high-temperature (UHT) treatment destroys all bacteria but not their spores. By law, milk, liquid egg and ice-cream mix must be either pasteurised, UHT treated or sterilised before they are sold.

Most milk is pasteurised– it should be stored in the refrigerator

UHT milk and canned goods may be stored at room temperature

Most canned foods are sterilised so that they can be stored for long periods of time at temperatures within the danger zone (8°C–63°C) until they are opened.

Date marking

Food labelling regulations introduced on 1 January 1991 make it compulsory for most foods to carry a date mark. The date mark indicates the date before which the food will be at its best to eat, if it has been stored correctly. It can be in one of three forms:

1. For foods that keep for three months or less: 'BEST BEFORE' followed by the day and month.
2. For foods that keep for more than three months: 'BEST BEFORE END' followed by the month and year.
3. For highly perishable foods – that is, those likely to cause illness if not eaten in the recommended time: 'USE BY' followed by the day and month. It is an offence to sell food for consumption after the 'use by' date.

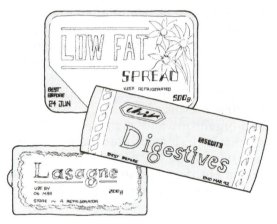

Always observe the date marks on manufactured foods

Any special storage conditions necessary should appear after each date mark, e.g., 'store in a refrigerator'.

Storage of food at low temperatures

Refrigeration

All foods that support bacterial growth must be kept in a refrigerator for short-term storage. These include:

*   raw meat and poultry
*   fresh fish including shellfish

- cooked meat, cooked fish and foods containing them as ingredients, e.g., pies, soups, stocks and gravy
- milk, cream, cheese, eggs and foods containing them as ingredients, e.g., quiches, trifles and cream cakes
- cooked rice.

Operating temperatures

The temperature inside a refrigerator should be kept between 1°C and 4°C. This will ensure that the temperature in the centre of the food stored in it is below 8°C (as demanded by law). A thermometer should be kept in the refrigerator and the temperature should be checked at least daily during the time when the refrigerator is most in use. The thermostat may need altering during periods of warm weather.

	COLD			CHILL			WARM		
LCD	28	32	36	39	43	46	50	54	°F
REFRIGERATOR THERMOMETER	-2	0	2	4	6	8	10	12	°C

Check the temperature of the refrigerator at regular intervals

Provided care is taken to maintain this temperature, most food poisoning bacteria, present in food being stored in the refrigerator, will be dormant. *Listeria monocytogenes* (see p. 94) is an exception in this respect as it can grow at a temperature of 4°C or less, although at a much slower rate than at room temperature. Spoilage bacteria, yeasts and moulds can also grow slowly at temperatures below 4°C, so although foods will deteriorate when they are kept in a refrigerator, this will occur more slowly than if they were kept at room temperature. The recommended maximum storage times for some common foods are as follows:

Food	Maximum storage time in a refrigerator (days)
Joints, chops, steaks	3–5
Poultry	2–3
Minced meat	1–2
Sausages	2–3
Bacon	7–10
Cooked meat	2–3
Raw fish	1–2
Shellfish	1
Cooked fish	2–3
Milk and cream	3–4
Eggs	14

Rules for keeping the temperature of the refrigerator and the food in it between 1°C and 4°C

Food must not be packed into a refrigerator too tightly.

Hot foods must be cooled before they are put in a refrigerator.

Provided it is used correctly, the refrigerator is a powerful weapon in the fight against food poisoning

1. Place the refrigerator in a well-ventilated area away from cooking appliances and out of direct sunlight.
2. Keep the door shut whenever possible. On a warm day, the temperature of a refrigerator can rise from 3°C to 10°C if the door is left open for 20 seconds.
3. Cool hot foods to a temperature of 15°C or below before placing them in the refrigerator.
4. Do not pack food too tightly into the refrigerator. There must be enough room around the food for the cold air to circulate.
5. Defrost the refrigerator regularly to prevent the build-up of ice around the refrigerating coils, as this reduces their efficiency.
6. Do not allow the temperature of the refrigerator to drop below 1°C because ice crystals will form in the food causing loss of texture and quality.

Cross-contamination

Ideally, raw foods should be kept in a separate refrigerator from high-risk foods so that cross-contamination cannot occur. If only one refrigerator is available, the positioning of foods should be carefully

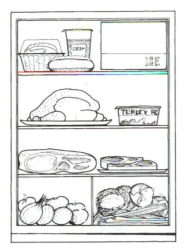

Raw meat must always be stored below cooked food

planned. Raw food must always be placed at the bottom of the refrigerator, with cooked food above it, so that any contaminated liquids from raw food cannot drip on to food that will not be cooked again.

Food should be covered while in the refrigerator to prevent cross-contamination, drying out and absorption of odours. If cling film is used for this purpose, it should only be placed over the food when it is cold. If the food is still warm, condensation collects on the food and the extra moisture accelerates the growth of spoilage bacteria and moulds. Cling film should not be allowed to touch the food it is covering and should not be used to wrap foods, particularly those that have a high fat content, e.g., cheese.

Stock rotation
Most foods now carry a 'best before' or a 'use by' date. Any foods that do not carry such a date should be coded when they are put in the refrigerator to ensure effective stock rotation. Older food must always be used first and any food that has been stored longer than the recommended time should be destroyed.

Cleaning
The refrigerator must be kept clean and any spills wiped up immediately. The inside surfaces should be washed regularly with a weak solution of sodium bicarbonate.

Refrigerated display cabinets
In many catering establishments, refrigerators with glass doors are used to display food such as desserts and cream cakes. It is very

important to check the temperature inside such cabinets regularly (several times a day on hot sunny days) to ensure that it does not rise above 4°C. If the glass door is exposed to sunlight, it will allow heat to build up in the same way as it does in a greenhouse. In addition, the fluorescent tubes used for display lighting will also tend to increase the temperature.

Chillers
Large catering premises may have a 'walk in' chilling room that contains a refrigeration unit and a fan to circulate the air. Small chillers are also available. Chillers are used to reduce the temperature of large volumes of meat or other food to 15°C or below within 1½ hours of cooking. The food can then be transferred to a refrigerator without risk of increasing the temperature of the refrigerator significantly.

Freezers

Freezers are widely used in catering premises, as well as in the home, for long-term, low-temperature storage of food. The majority of bacteria will survive the freezing process and can remain dormant for months or years in the frozen food, although they are unable to multiply. Freezing therefore cannot improve the quality of contaminated food, so only fresh, good quality food should be put in a freezer.

When frozen food is thawed, any dormant bacteria start to grow and multiply again when the temperature reaches the danger zone (8°C–63°C), so it is important to thaw food in the correct way (see p. 33).

Operating temperatures
A star marking system has been devised to indicate the temperature in a freezer or in the frozen food storage compartment of a refrigerator. A four star symbol distinguishes a true freezer from appliances that are only designed to store frozen food. The operation temperature of a

	Temperature of freezer	Food storage time
✻	–6°C (21°F)	1 week
✻✻	–12°C (10°F)	1 month
✻✻✻	–18°C (0°F)	3 months
✻ ✻✻✻	–18°C (0°F) to –25°C (–15°F)	3 months or longer; capable of freezing fresh food

four star freezer is also –18°C, but in addition to its storage use it is capable of freezing fresh food without affecting the temperature of the frozen food in the rest of the freezer.

Storage times

The bacteria that cause food poisoning cannot multiply in or on frozen food, so provided that the temperature of the freezer is maintained at –18°C there is no danger of frozen food becoming a health hazard, however long it is stored. The taste, colour and texture of the food will, however, deteriorate, so recommended storage times refer to the length of time the food can be stored without any change in its eating quality. The flavour of foods with a high fat content tends to deteriorate more quickly than that of other foods. Since people's opinions about the flavour of food vary, opinions about storage times will also vary. As a guide, the following table gives some storage times for foods stored in a four star freezer:

Food	*Freezer* Storage time (months)
Beef	12
Lamb and veal	9
Pork	6
Mince, offal, sausages	3
Pâté	1
Chicken and turkey	12
Duck and game birds	6
Giblets	3
White fish	6
Oily fish	3
Shellfish	2
Bread and cakes	6
Fruit	9
Vegetables	12
Ice cream	3

Blast freezers

Commercially prepared frozen food is frozen in a blast freezer. The blast freezer is a chamber with a continuous blast of cold air at –20°C circulating through it. This provides a very rapid method of freezing and gives a better quality product than a domestic freezer. Some large catering establishments have a blast freezer.

Open-top display freezers

Open-top display freezers are not intended to be used for freezing food; they are only intended for storing it before sale. Storage times

may be different from those shown for a domestic freezer, so the manufacturers' recommendations should be observed. Food must never be
stored above the freezer load line, since the temperature here will be
higher than that in the main freezer compartment.

Freezer breakdown

If the freezer breaks down or there is a power cut, the food should be
left inside the freezer, the door or lid kept shut and blankets placed
over it. If the freezer is tightly packed, the food will probably remain
frozen for 24 hours or longer. If the food is still partially frozen when
the freezer is mended, it may be safe to keep it, but only if the surface
temperature of the food is less than 8°C. Alternatively, some foods can
be cooked and refrozen. If there is any doubt, an environmental health
officer should be contacted to advise about the various options.

Points to remember about freezers and frozen food

The delivery temperature of frozen food must not be higher than –15°C

- The delivery temperature of frozen food should always be checked.
  Temperatures above –15°C are unacceptable.
- Frozen food should always be wrapped to prevent cross-
  contamination and freezer burn.
- A tightly packed freezer is neater and more economical to run. Once
  food is frozen, cold air does not need to circulate, as it does in a
  refrigerator.
- New stock should always be marked with the date when it is placed
  in the freezer and stored underneath old stock. Regular stock checks
  should be made on the freezer contents to ensure that older stock is
  used before newer stock.
- The temperature of the freezer should be checked regularly.

- Food should not be refrozen once it has thawed for two reasons: any food poisoning bacteria present will have multiplied if the food has been kept at a temperature within the danger zone for any length of time; when food is refrozen relatively slowly in domestic freezers, large ice crystals form which result in a noticeable loss of texture when the food is thawed again. If the food is cooked after thawing, it may be refrozen.

Storage of food at room temperature

Dry food stores

All foods that do not require refrigerated storage, such as rice, flour, pulses, canned foods, fresh fruit and vegetables, should be stored in a room that is cool, dry, clean, well lit and ventilated. If possible, fruit and vegetables should be stored separately from dry goods.

Storage rooms should be designed so that pests and insects cannot enter them easily. As an additional precaution, all open food in the store should be covered and placed above floor level on tubular or

A dry food store

mesh shelves, so that if any pests do enter the store, they will not have easy access to the food. To prevent insect pests from reaching the food by climbing up the wall, shelves and storage racks should not be in contact with the walls. Any spillages should be wiped up immediately.

Stock rotation is very important. If the packets and cans in the store do not have a date mark, some method of marking must be devised to ensure that old stock is used before newer stock.

Rice, flour and pulses
Foods such as these that are not pre-packed should be stored in mobile metal bins with tight-fitting lids.

Fruit and vegetables
Any plastic wrapping on fruit and vegetables should be removed before they are put in the store because it traps condensation, which encourages mould growth. Mould spreads rapidly, so mouldy fruit and vegetables should be thrown away immediately. Fruit and vegetables should be used as soon as possible after delivery.

Canned foods
Food poisoning from canned foods is very rare, although changes in colour, texture and flavour of the food will take place if cans are kept too long. The shelf-life of acid canned foods is shorter than that of neutral foods. As a guide, here are some storage times for some common canned foods:

Food	Storage time (months)
Rhubarb, grapefruit	9
Fruit juices, milk products	12
Other fruit, potatoes, baked beans, tomato products	18
Vegetables, soups	24
Solid pack meat* and fish in oil	60

* Some catering-sized cans of ham are only pasteurised to avoid shrinkage of the ham and to maintain its flavour. The canned ham is not free from micro-organisms and must be stored in a refrigerator. The manufacturers' instructions, which should appear on the label, must be followed.

Once a can has been opened, the contents must be treated as fresh food. Any unused food should be emptied into a plastic or glass container, otherwise it will absorb tin from the can, particularly if it is an acid food. High-risk food from a can must be stored in a refrigerator once the can has been opened.

Some cans develop a bulge on storage. These cans, which are known as 'blown' cans, must not be used. The gas that causes the bulge may

Do not use blown or dented cans

have been produced by bacteria, indicating that the can has not been properly sterilised. Alternatively, the gas may have been produced in a chemical reaction inside the can. If the lacquer inside the can is damaged, tin and iron from the can will also have been absorbed by the food. High levels of metals in food cause severe vomiting. This type of chemical poisoning usually occurs in acid foods that have been stored for longer than the manufacturers' recommendations. Any other cans from the same batch (as indicated by the code on the end of the can) should not be used without discussing the problem with the manufacturer or an environmental health officer. Rusty or badly dented cans, particularly those where the dent occurs on or near the seam, must not be used. It is possible that the dent will have caused a very tiny opening along the can seam, allowing micro-organisms to enter.

Storage of food at high temperatures

If food is to be served within a short time of preparation, it will probably be more convenient to store it hot, rather than cooling and reheating it again. Most commercial kitchens use a hot cupboard, heated by gas or electricity, or a bain-marie, which is a heated well, filled with hot water, to keep food hot ready for service. Such devices must be preheated before putting hot food in them, so that the temperature at the centre of the food is kept above 63°C and bacterial multiplication cannot take place.

Cold food must not be reheated by putting it in either a hot cupboard or a bain-marie as the heating process would be too slow and would allow extensive bacterial growth.

Case History

From a party of 43 children and 5 adults on a summer outing, 20 children became ill with severe diarrhoea and vomiting the day after the trip. A picnic lunch was provided on the trip which consisted of a roast chicken joint, a slice of quiche, salad and a bread roll, followed by a packet of sweet biscuits and an apple. On examination of a sample of the picnic meal, the chicken portion was found to be heavily contaminated with *Salmonella* bacteria. Investigations revealed that the chicken joints had been cooked the day before the trip. They were removed from the oven by a chef who had been cracking eggs to make the quiche. He removed the chicken joints from the baking tray by hand, piled them on top of each other in a large plastic container and put the container in the refrigerator. The next day, each chicken portion was put on an individual polystyrene tray, together with the quiche, salad and a bread roll. The trays were covered with foil and packed into cardboard boxes ready for transportation.

1. The chicken joints are transferred by hand from the baking tray to a plastic container.

2. They are put in the refrigerator without being cooled.

3. The children eat their picnic.

4. Many of the children become ill with severe diarrhoea and vomiting.

Faults

1. The chicken joints were not cooled to 15°C or below before they were put in the refrigerator.
2. The chicken joints should not have been piled on top of each other. This stops cold air from circulating around them.
3. The cooked chicken joints were cross-contaminated probably via the chef's hands.
4. The food was not transported in a cool box.

Chapter 7
Kitchen Design and Equipment

The industrial kitchen

Design

A well-planned, easily cleaned kitchen will save time and effort in food preparation and will reduce the risk of contaminating food.

Allow plenty of space for food preparation and storage

The most hygienic kitchen layout is one that allows plenty of space for food preparation and storage, and one where there is a continuous progression of food from delivery through preparation and cooking to the finished product.

Preparation areas should be well lit to help to prevent accidents and to show up any dirt on the work surface and equipment. Tables should stand well away from the wall to allow for cleaning, or be built into the wall with the junction between the table and the wall sealed.

Preparation areas can have their own built-in cooking equipment, although it is often more convenient to have a central cooking island

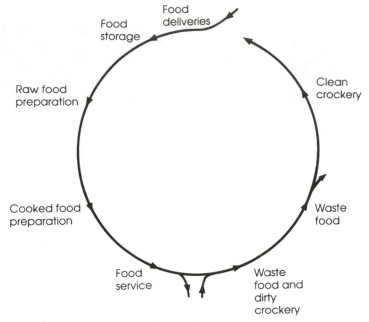

There should be a continuous progression of food from its delivery to service of the cooked product

with ventilation ducts immediately above it to keep the kitchen temperature as near to normal room temperature as possible.

An example of a satisfactory layout for a kitchen serving a restaurant is shown in the diagram opposite. This layout can be varied depending on the size and shape of the kitchen and the type of meals being prepared. In this example kitchen, consideration has been given to the following points to prevent cross-contamination:

- The vegetable preparation area is near the delivery door so that dust and soil from fresh vegetables do not contaminate cooked food.
- The raw meat preparation area is well separated from the cooked food preparation area, since raw meat is almost always contaminated with food poisoning bacteria. In a large industrial kitchen, there should be some physical barrier between the raw meat and cooked food handling areas.
- Storage rooms are near the delivery door.
- The servery doors divide the food preparation area from the washing-up area. Plates should be scraped clean immediately after use and put through the washing process before being stored ready for reuse.

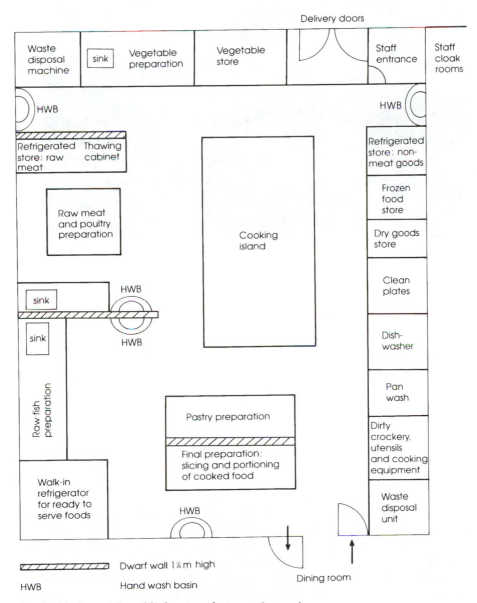

A suitable layout for a kitchen serving a restaurant

A modern industrial kitchen

Construction materials

The materials used in the construction of a kitchen must have certain properties, bearing in mind the almost constant use they will have during working hours. A summary of these is given in the following check-list. Note, in particular, that wood should not be used anywhere in a kitchen as it is very absorbent, which makes it almost impossible to clean thoroughly. It also splinters and cracks easily, providing harbourage for bacteria.

Area of kitchen	Qualities required	Suitable materials
Work surfaces	Hard wearing	Food-grade stainless steel
	Easy to clean	
	Non-absorbent	
	Resistant to acids, fat, grease and cleaning chemicals	
	Resistant to impact and heat	
Walls	Smooth	Well-grouted, glazed ceramic tiles
	Non-absorbent	Stainless steel sheets
	Non-flaking	Steam-resistant emulsion (above 1.5 m (5 ft))
	Light coloured	
	Easy to clean	
Floors	Durable	Non-slip quarry tiles laid in acid-resisting cement
	Easy to clean	
	Non-absorbent	Thick non-slip vinyl sheets
	Non-slip	
	Resistant to acids, fat and grease	
	Coved at the junction with the wall	
Ceilings	Fire resistant	Stove-enamelled metal tiles
	Smooth	Plasterboard sheeting (coved to wall)
	Light coloured	
	Easy to clean	

Toilet and washing facilities

Each catering establishment must provide an adequate number of toilets and washing facilities for its employees. Except in very small establishments, these should not be the same ones used by customers. The toilets must not lead straight into a food room but should be separated from it by a well-ventilated corridor.

Ideally, toilets should have foot-operated flushes. Since hand-washing after using the toilet is so important, it should be impossible for anyone to leave the toilet without passing a wash basin. By law, a notice requesting people to wash their hands must be displayed. Hot and cold water, liquid bactericidal soap, a nailbrush and paper towels,

Modern hand-washing facilities

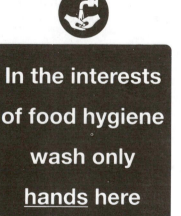

In the interests of food hygiene wash only <u>hands</u> here

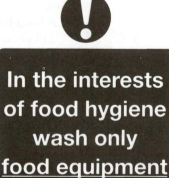

In the interests of food hygiene wash only <u>food equipment</u> here

a roller towel or a hot air dryer must be provided at all hand-wash basins. To maintain high standards of personal cleanliness, one person should be made responsible for ensuring that toilets are kept clean and that wash basins have all the necessary supplies. The liquid soap containers should be cleaned, disinfected, refilled and replaced as soon as they are empty; nailbrushes should be cleaned and disinfected each day; paper towels should be topped up when necessary and roller towels replaced as soon as they come to the end.

Wash basins must also be provided in the food preparation room at convenient locations. Ideally, they should have foot-operated taps, since these are more hygienic than hand-operated taps. At least one wash basin should be present near the entrance to the kitchen, to encourage food handlers to wash their hands before starting food preparation. Sinks with hot and cold water should be located in each preparation area for washing food, and these must not be used for hand-washing. If a sink is to be used only for washing fish, vegetables or fruit, a supply of cold water is sufficient.

Waste disposal

Waste food must be removed from the food preparation area as soon as possible. Wet refuse can be disposed of quickly and efficiently in a waste disposal unit – this shreds the waste and flushes it into the drainage system. Waste disposal units can either be free standing or built into the sink unit.

If there is no mechanical waste disposal unit, strong plastic or paper sacks can be used. When these are full, they should be sealed and removed straight away to an outside dustbin. They should always be emptied at the end of the day, whether they are full or not, because

A free-standing waste disposal unit

A plastic refuse sack

A large wheeled bin used for refuse disposal

waste food provides an excellent source of food for pests. A well-planned kitchen will have several waste disposal points so that waste food does not have to be carried through cooked food preparation areas.

The outside refuse area should be a specially designed area that is easily reached from the kitchen but is not too near the door or a window, since refuse tends to attract flies and wasps in the summer. It should have a concrete surrounding wall and a concrete floor, as well as a water supply point so that it can be hosed down regularly to keep it clean. Sacks of waste brought to this area from the kitchen should be stored in plastic or steel bins or large wheeled containers until they are collected. All bins must have tight-fitting lids that will not be blown off by the wind or knocked off by animals. The bins must never be allowed to overflow. Arrangements must be made with the local authority or a contract agency for frequent collection of refuse so that it does not accumulate and cause a health hazard. The bins should be cleaned and disinfected regularly after emptying.

It is very important that food handlers wash their hands after handling refuse, before starting food preparation again.

The domestic kitchen

Many of the considerations necessary when planning the layout of an industrial kitchen are also relevant to the domestic kitchen:

- A well-organised, clean kitchen with good lighting and ventilation is an important factor in the prevention of food poisoning.
- Where possible, a separate work surface and separate equipment should be used for the preparation of raw meat and cooked foods. If this is not possible, the work surface and equipment should be thoroughly cleaned after handling raw meat and before its use for cooked food.
- Due attention should be paid to the disposal of waste to ensure that it is not a source of contamination in the kitchen.

Case History

A small hotel on the south coast was found to be responsible for an outbreak of food poisoning affecting 52 people. A midsummer dance was held at the hotel, at which a buffet supper was provided during the evening. Between 12 and 18 hours after the meal, 52 out of the 90 people at the dance became ill with severe diarrhoea, abdominal pains and vomiting. The buffet meal had consisted of roast chicken, roast beef and roast ham with a variety of salads.

1. The chef used the same table to prepare raw and cooked food.

2. Much of the food was left at room temperature.

3. The buffet supper was eaten at 10 p.m.

4. The next day many of those who had eaten the supper became ill with severe diarrhoea and vomiting.

Investigations revealed that the kitchens were very cramped and normally only catered for 30 people. There were two preparation tables: one for raw food and one for cooked food. However, because of the extra volume of food to be prepared, the chef had used the same table for preparing the raw meat and for slicing and arranging the cooked meat on serving dishes. He used a damp cloth to wipe the table when necessary. There was no wash basin in the kitchen, so it is possible that the cooked meat was cross-contaminated from the raw meat via the chef's hands. There was insufficient refrigeration space, so some of the food prepared during the day was left at room temperature until the evening.

Faults

1. The kitchen did not have adequate facilities (including refrigeration space) to cater for 90 people.
2. Juices from raw meat were allowed to come into contact with cooked meat.
3. Preparation surfaces and equipment were not cleaned thoroughly between each preparation stage.
4. There was no wash basin in the kitchen.

Chapter 8
Cleaning and Disinfection

Cleaning is never a popular task but there are many reasons for maintaining a clean kitchen. Apart from making it a more pleasant place in which to work, a clean kitchen will help to prevent the contamination of food and will also reduce the risk of pest infestation. Premises can be closed down and fines of up to £20 000 can be imposed if the premises are so dirty that they present a health hazard.

A clean kitchen will help to prevent the contamination of food during its preparation

Cleaning schedules

It is important to establish a cleaning routine. The 'clean as you go' rule is essential for preparation surfaces and equipment that come into direct contact with food. All food handlers should be responsible for cleaning the surfaces and equipment as and when they use them.

Cleaning Schedule			
Equipment	Frequency	Method	Person responsible
Work surfaces	After each use	Wash with hot water and detergent. Apply a solution of disinfectant. Leave 3 minutes. Rinse. Air dry.	Everybody
Floors	Daily	Wash with hot water and detergent. Rinse. Air dry.	P.J. Scott
Walls, doors, paintwork	Weekly	Wash with hot water and detergent. Rinse. Air dry.	A.R. Thompson
Tiles behind sinks, work surfaces	Daily	Wash with hot water and detergent. Rinse. Air dry.	R.S. Dalgleish

Cleaning schedule

Other areas of the kitchen and larger equipment should be cleaned on a regular basis. To ensure that nothing is overlooked, a cleaning schedule should be devised. The cleaning schedule should be displayed in the kitchen, listing the items to be cleaned, the frequency and method of cleaning, and the name of the person responsible for doing the task.

Cleaning materials

The three main cleaning agents are:

- detergents
- disinfectants
- hot water.

Detergents

Detergents are chemicals that, when added to water, help to remove grease, dirt and food residues. They do not, however, kill bacteria. Detergents are more effective when used with hot water. Washing-up liquid is a detergent that is used in the home and in industrial kitchens to clean utensils and most equipment but its action is fairly mild – other detergents are available for heavily soiled equipment. A very alkaline detergent is used in dishwashers and can be used for removing baked-on grease from kitchen equipment.

Disinfectants

Disinfectants are chemicals that kill the majority of bacteria but do not destroy spores. Although not all bacteria are destroyed, the number present on disinfected equipment is reduced to a level that is safe for food preparation. Disinfectants will only be effective if the equipment has already had grease and food residues removed by washing with hot water and a detergent.

Hypochlorites

Although a variety of chemical disinfectants are available, hypochlorites (more commonly known as bleach) are probably the most widely used in the catering industry for disinfecting surfaces and equipment. They are inexpensive and, provided that they are used at the correct dilution, are very effective, leaving little taste or smell. To be effective, hypochlorites must be left in contact with the equipment being disinfected for a specific time, called the 'contact time'. The main disadvantage of hypochlorites is that they are easily inactivated by food particles, so they are only effective when the equipment has already been thoroughly cleaned with hot water and a detergent.

Hot water

Chemical disinfectants are not always necessary. The use of water at a temperature of approximately 80°C or steam is a very effective method of disinfection, and is preferable to chemical disinfection because there is no risk of contaminating food with chemicals. In instances where the use of nearly boiling water is not practical, a chemical disinfectant is used instead.

Sanitisers

Sanitisers are chemicals that combine both a detergent and a disinfectant. In theory, one application of a sanitiser should remove dirt and kill micro-organisms, but in practice they tend to be less effective than a detergent wash followed by disinfection. They are only suitable for lightly soiled surfaces.

Surfaces requiring disinfection

Not all surfaces and equipment in a kitchen need to be disinfected. Often, a detergent wash is sufficient. Disinfection after cleaning is normally considered necessary for:

- work surfaces in direct contact with food
- the hands of food handlers
- equipment touched by food handlers during preparation, e.g., refrigerator door handles
- cleaning materials and equipment.

Hand disinfection

Hand disinfection is particularly important for food handlers preparing high-risk foods and for those who handle both raw meat and ready-to-eat foods during the day. Some soaps called bactericidal soaps include a disinfectant. Alternatively, a cream containing a disinfectant can be rubbed into the hands after washing with liquid soap. Apart from its disinfecting properties, the cream will help to prevent the hands from becoming rough and cracked, and hence from harbouring bacteria.

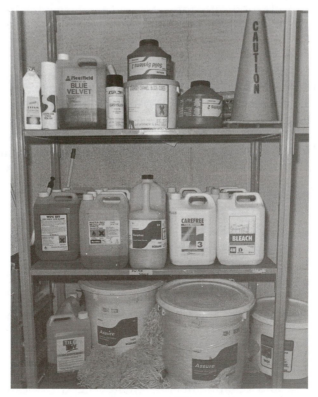

Cleaning chemicals must be stored away from food

Storage of cleaning agents

All chemicals must be kept away from food. A dry, cool, well-ventilated and well-lit room that can be locked should be used to store them. Containers must be stored firmly closed in an upright position and must be clearly labelled. If chemicals are bought in bulk and decanted into smaller containers, a label giving details of the chemical and its use must be put on the new container. Empty food and drink containers must not be used for storage of chemicals because of the risk of their contents being mistaken.

If chemicals have to be diluted down before use, a sink, water supply and work surface should be present in the store. When preparing cleaning solutions, it is very important to follow the manufacturer's instructions about dilution rates. Making a more concentrated solution could cause damage to surfaces, is wasteful and is unlikely to improve the performance of the cleaning agent. On the other hand, a too dilute solution is likely to be ineffective. A fresh disinfectant solution must be made up for each task because dirt inactivates disinfectants.

Under no circumstances should anyone attempt to make their own cleaning agents – some cleaning chemicals when mixed together give off poisonous gases.

It is dangerous to mix some types of cleaning chemicals

The cleaning process

The basic principles of the cleaning process are the same whether it is cutlery, utensils, equipment, surfaces or floors that are being cleaned. The process can be divided into five stages.

The five stages of the cleaning process

1. Removal of food residues.
2. Washing with hot water and a detergent.
3. Rinsing to remove dirt and detergent.
4. Disinfection with either hot water or a chemical.
5. Drying.

Dishwashing

Dishwashing can be done either by hand or machine. If items are to be washed by hand, two sinks should be used, one for washing and one

The 'two-sink' method of dishwashing by hand

for rinsing and disinfecting. The following procedure should be followed:

1. Scrape off left over food and rinse in warm water if necessary. (Stage 1 of the cleaning process)
2. Place the items to be washed in hot water (50°C–60°C) and detergent and remove any food residues by scrubbing with a nylon brush. Dishcloths harbour bacteria and should not be used. (Stage 2 of the cleaning process)
3. Place the items in the second sink in very hot water (75°C–82°C) for approximately two minutes. This will remove any detergent and disinfect them, as well as making them hot enough to dry quickly when removed from the sink. (Stages 3 and 4 of the cleaning process)
4. Remove the items from the rinsing water and leave to drain in a clean rack until they are completely dry, when they should be removed and stored in a clean, dry area until required for use. If items are to be dried by hand, disposable paper towels should be used rather than tea towels, as tea towels quickly become contaminated. (Stage 5 of the cleaning process)

It is very important to maintain the correct temperatures in both the washing and rinsing sinks. To do this, it will be necessary to change the

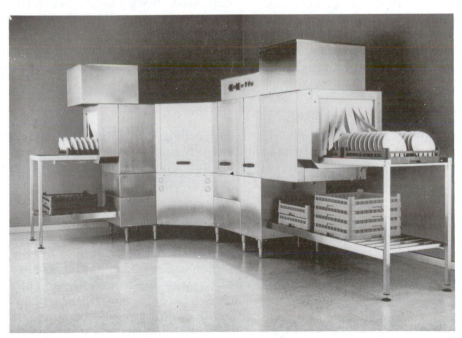

Dishwashing machines provide a hygienic method of washing up

water frequently and add more detergent to the first sink. Rubber gloves should always be worn because if the temperature of the water is hot enough, it will be too hot for bare hands.

Dishwashing machines are now widely used both in catering establishments and in the home. They vary in design but all of them go through stages 1–5. In an industrial machine, the items to be washed are loaded on to a moving belt, which then passes through the machine. In domestic machines, they are loaded into racks. Cups, glasses and jugs must be stacked upside down so that water does not collect in them, and cutlery should be placed with the dirty end uppermost. Dishwashing machines provide a hygienic method of washing up, provided they have regular maintenance and the temperature of the washing and rinsing cycle is correct. Most industrial machines have temperature dials on the outside so that the operator can check the temperature of the washing and rinsing water.

Cleaning the kitchen

Work surfaces
Any surface that will come into contact with food, especially food that will not be cooked again, must be kept scrupulously clean. Work surfaces should be cleaned with hot water and detergent after each use and then disinfected with either hot water or a chemical. Any traces of a chemical disinfectant must be removed with a final rinse. The surfaces should be thoroughly dried with disposable paper towels – wet surfaces will encourage the growth of micro-organisms.

Walls, doors and ceilings
Regular cleaning of walls, doors and ceilings with hot water and a detergent is sufficient to stop grease building up on these surfaces. Areas behind sinks, work surfaces and cooking apparatus where splashes occur will require very frequent cleaning.

Floors
Floors quickly become contaminated and must be cleaned at least daily. Where possible, kitchen equipment should be built in or mobile, but if it is not, care must be taken to clean under and behind it. Electric floor scrubbers are a quick and effective way of cleaning floors, but if no machine is available, floors will have to be washed by hand using hot water and a suitable detergent. If possible, floors should be coned off during cleaning because slippery floors are a hazard. They will air dry quickly, as long as the water used is hot enough.

Equipment

All equipment and utensils used in food premises should be easy to clean and disinfect. Large equipment should be easy to dismantle and reassemble so that the parts that come into contact with food can be cleaned thoroughly and disinfected.

Any cracked or chipped plates, glasses or equipment should be discarded because even an efficient washing-up process will not remove bacteria from the cracks.

Wood chopping boards, knife handles, mixing spoons and rolling pins should be avoided as wood absorbs moisture and is almost impossible to clean thoroughly. Kitchen equipment is available made from plastic laminates or other synthetic materials, and these are much more suitable for food preparation.

Case History

A restaurant was found to be responsible for a series of cases of food poisoning. The restaurant in question was known for its regular 'Tudor Evenings'. The meal provided at these events consisted of a large steak together with a selection of salads, all of which were served on a wooden platter.

On investigation, it was found that the wooden platters, many of which were scored and cracked, were scraped clean after use and washed by hand. The person responsible for doing the washing up did not wear rubber gloves and so the temperature of the water was unlikely to be at the recommended temperature of 50°C–60°C. There was no second sink for rinsing and disinfecting. To prepare for the evening, the staff at the restaurant plated up the salads on the wooden platters during the day and left them on a large table, ready for the freshly cooked steak to be added later in the evening. Some of the salads contained high-risk ingredients, such as rice and egg, and many were dressed in mayonnaise. Although no foods were available for analysis, it was assumed that the salads were being cross-contaminated from the wooden platters. As a result, the restaurant was asked to discontinue the use of the wooden platters.

1. Wooden equipment was used for the service of food.

2. The washing-up process was very unsatisfactory.

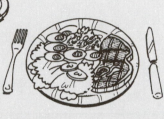

3. High-risk foods were left at room temperature for a long period of time.

Faults

1. Wooden equipment was used for the service of food.
2. The washing-up process was very unsatisfactory.
3. Salads containing high-risk ingredients were left at room temperature for a long period of time.

Chapter 9
Pest Control

Pest infestations are one of the major reasons for prosecutions in the catering industry. The Food Safety Act 1990 gives environmental health officers the power to close down premises immediately if there is a serious pest infestation. Fines of up to £5000 and/or a 6 month prison sentence can also be imposed.

There are three main groups of pests commonly found in food premises:

- Rodents: mainly rats and mice.
- Insects: mainly flies and cockroaches.
- Birds: mainly sparrows, pigeons and starlings.

Problems associated with pests

- All pests carry food poisoning bacteria in their droppings, and also on their fur, feathers and feet. They therefore contaminate the food they eat, any exposed food they climb over and any work surfaces that they run over.
- Rats and mice need to wear down their incisor teeth which grow continuously. To do this, they gnaw woodwork, gas and water pipes, and electric cables, often with disastrous consequences.
- Cockroaches leave a characteristic and very unpleasant smell. They like warm, moist areas where they will be undisturbed and are often found behind ovens and hot water pipes. They are able to squeeze through very narrow gaps. They generally emerge only when it is dark.
- Flies feed on a wide variety of matter including infected waste food and animal faeces. They pick up large numbers of food poisoning bacteria which they transfer to human food when they land on it. While they are feeding, they deposit faeces on the food. They also vomit saliva on to the food to digest it partially before sucking it up again.
- Bird droppings make buildings look dirty and ugly; they can also damage the structure of the building. Bird nests block gutters, causing overflows which may lead to structural damage.

Some common pests

Prevention

Pests are attracted to food premises that provide them with food, water, warmth and shelter. All pests breed rapidly if they are provided with these conditions. For example, a female mouse can produce 60 offspring per year. Each of these will begin to breed when it is only two months old. The female housefly lays four to six batches of between 100 and 150 eggs during her adult life of one to three months.

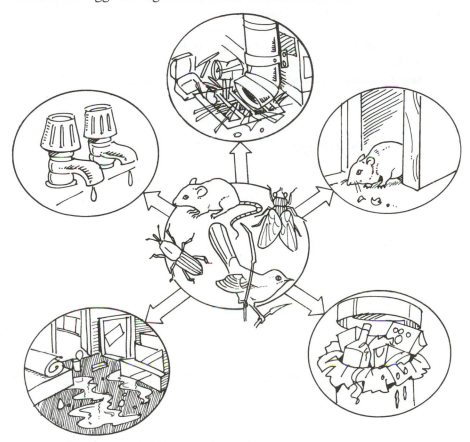

Pests are attracted to premises that provide food, water and shelter

To stop pests from entering catering premises, it is important to keep the buildings in good repair, and to keep doors shut and windows closed or covered with fly screens. As pests often enter the kitchen in food containers, all deliveries should be checked before being taken into the kitchen. Rats drink three times as much as they eat and will not stay in premises where water is unavailable. It is important therefore to mend dripping taps and defective gutters as soon as they are spotted.

Despite taking all these steps, pests may still find a way into the building. The following precautions must be taken to prevent them from breeding and establishing themselves.

Ways to prevent pest infestation

- Keep all food covered during storage.
- Keep waste food in covered refuse bins.
- Ensure that food preparation areas are thoroughly cleaned at the end of the working day.
- Store food off the floor and away from walls.
- Implement a cleaning schedule which includes areas behind equipment and ceiling cavities.

Signs of infestation

Food handlers should not try to deal with pest infestations themselves, but they must be able to recognise when pests are present so that they can call in professional help immediately. The following are all signs of an infestation:

- live or dead rodents, insects or birds
- droppings
- gnawing marks
- torn packets, paper sacks or cardboard boxes
- grease marks on skirting boards
- footprints in dust.

Control of pests

In any kitchen where flies are likely to be a problem, an electrically operated fly killer should be fitted. This consists of an ultraviolet light that attracts flies and other flying insects to a metal grid with an electric current running through it. The flies are electrocuted when they touch the metal grid and fall into a collecting tray underneath. The tray must be emptied and cleaned on a regular basis to ensure that dead flies do not drop into food being prepared below.

Control of other pest infestations must be left to a qualified person. Expert advice can be obtained from the Environmental Health Department of the local authority or from a specialist organisation

A clean and tidy kitchen where no food is available will be unattractive to pests

Regular inspection and monitoring of food premises will prevent a pest infestation

such as Rentokil. Most professional pest control services offer an inspection and monitoring service, as well as a deep cleaning service to eliminate problems associated with pests before the pests have had time to establish themselves in a building.

However, if pests are present, a quick method of controlling them is necessary, and this is where chemical poisons are useful. The Control of Pesticides Regulations 1986 strictly control the pesticides that may be used for any particular purpose. Frequent use of chemical pesticides where food is being prepared is not desirable and the emphasis should always be on prevention rather than on control.

Rats and mice are usually eliminated with poisons (rodenticides) housed in tamper-resistant bait boxes, which reduces the risk of poisons getting into food products. Rats are very suspicious animals and baiting is necessary for at least two weeks before they will take the poisoned food.

Cockroach and other insect infestations are usually treated with insecticide sprays.

Birds are encouraged to eat food mixed with a narcotic drug that causes deep sleep. They are then removed and, if necessary, destroyed humanely. If any protected bird takes the bait, it is revived and released, none the worse for the experience.

Case History

Out of a total of 22 people dining at a small country restaurant one evening, nine people suffered from severe diarrhoea, vomiting and fever. The meals eaten had varied and there was no food that had been eaten by everybody. However, 16 people had eaten sweets from the trolley, including the nine people afflicted.

On investigation, it was found that sweets left over from the previous evening had not been thrown away but had been served again the following evening. The sweets had been left on the trolley, which had been left overnight in the store room. The store room was very untidy, with packets of food on the floor. The environmental health officer investigating the incident found all the traces of an infestation of mice: torn packets of flour, droppings and gnawing marks on the skirting boards. The proprietor was aware of the infestation and had laid mouse traps. The remainder of two sweets, both of which contained cream, were sent for analysis and were found to be heavily contaminated with bacteria.

1. Sweets remaining at the end of the evening were left on the trolley which was wheeled into the store room.

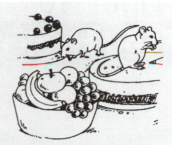

2. During the night, mice which were already present in the store room contaminated the food.

3. Customers were offered the sweets the next evening.

4. Over the next two days, most of the customers suffer from vomiting and diarrhoea.

Faults

1. Professional help was not sought at the first signs of a pest infestation.
2. Sweets containing cream were kept for many hours at room temperature.
3. Food was kept on the floor in the store room.

Chapter 10
Food Hygiene Legislation

Food Safety (General Food Hygiene) Regulations 1995

These regulations came into force on 15th September 1995 and are available from HMSO (SI 1995 No 1763). The Regulations aim to ensure that the same food hygiene rules are enforced in all European Union countries. Anyone who owns, manages or works in a food business must adhere to them. This includes people who transport, pack and store food, not just those who prepare it. All types of food businesses are included: anything from an expensive restaurant or large supermarket to a stall in a village hall or a vending machine.

The new regulations are in many ways similar to previous regulations but rather than being simply a list of rules, a greater emphasis is put on proprietors identifying the food safety hazards likely to arise in their particular business and devising procedures to control these risks ensuring that safe food is sold to the customer.

Requirements of the 1995 Food Safety Regulations

Food premises

Rooms where food is prepared, treated or processed should:
- be clean and maintained in good repair
- have surface finishes which are easy to clean and where necessary disinfect
- have an adequate supply of drinking water
- have adequate facilities, including hot and cold water, for washing food and equipment
- have adequate hand washing facilities
- have suitable controls in place to protect against pests
- have adequate natural and/or artificial light
- have sufficient natural and/or artificial ventilation. Filters must be accessible for cleaning
- provide clean lavatories which do not lead directly into food rooms.

These are the basic minimum hygiene standards for all food businesses. But, whether a surface is cleaned or disinfected and how often, will depend on whether it is being used for the preparation of high-risk or low-risk foods.

Food handlers

All food handlers must maintain a high standard of personal hygiene. They should:
- wash hands frequently when handling food
- wear clean overalls
- never smoke whilst preparing food
- report any illnesses particularly vomiting, diarrhoea and infected wounds to the manager.

All food handlers are expected to observe these rules. Again, the frequency of hand-washing will vary depending on whether high-risk or low-risk foods are being handled.

Training

All food handlers should be given some training to enable them to perform their particular job without any risk of causing food poisoning. More training will be necessary for caterers handling high-risk foods than for people dealing with packaged low-risk food. The owner of a food business is responsible for training his staff 'in-house' or sending them on a recognised course.

Food Safety (Temperature Control) Regulations 1995

All food likely to support the growth of pathogenic bacteria or the formation of toxins must be stored at a temperature below 8°C. If a food which would normally support the growth of micro-organisms is stored above 8°C, the owner of the food business must be able to offer a scientific assessment (a microbiological analysis by a qualified scientist) of the safety of the food under the conditions in which it is stored. If the food is to be served hot it must be kept at a temperature of 63°C or above. Food which is about to be served hot may be kept hot (but below 63°C) for a maximum period of two hours. Food which is about to be served cold may be kept at a temperature above 8°C for a maximum of four hours.

Food Safety Act 1990

This Act is concerned with the safety of food from farm production to the point when it is sold. It is an offence to sell or possess for sale food that:

- is unfit to eat either because it is contaminated with pathogenic micro-organisms or because it contains poisonous chemicals or foreign bodies
- has false or misleading labelling or advertisement.

Two important provisions of the Food Safety Act 1990 are:

1. Registration of premises
Food premises including mobile premises such as hamburger vans must be registered with their local district council at least 28 days before trading begins. This gives the Environmental Health Officer opportunity to inspect the premises and give Food Safety advice where necessary. There is no charge for registration.

2. Emergency closure
Environmental health officers are allowed to close premises without notice if there is an immediate danger to public health.

Inspection of premises

Environmental health officers inspect all food businesses on a regular basis and will make extra visits if there is any reason to suspect that premises or practices are unhygienic. Apart from enforcing legislation environmental health officers are available to give advice and guidance on any matter relating to food hygiene.

After an inspection the environmental health officer might write informally to the proprietor of the business asking him to put right any problems which have come to light during the inspection. If the offences are more serious he may take one of the following actions:

- issue an *Improvement Notice*, which requests that certain measures are taken to comply with food hygiene legislation. A specified time limit is set for the improvements to be made (this will be at least a fortnight).
- prosecute the proprietor for a breach of the food hygiene regulations. If the court feels that public health is at risk, it will impose a *Prohibition Order*, which closes all or the part of the business that does not comply with the regulations.
- issue an *Emergency Prohibition Notice*. If the offence imposes an

immediate risk to public health, the environmental health officer can close the premises immediately for three days by issuing an Emergency Prohibition Notice. The matter is taken before a court within the three days. If the court agrees that the offence imposes an immediate risk to health, it will issue an *Emergency Prohibition Order*, which keeps the premises closed until the necessary improvements have been made.

To lift a Prohibition Order or an Emergency Prohibition Order, to re-open the premises, the proprietor must apply to the environmental health officer for a *Certificate of Satisfaction.*

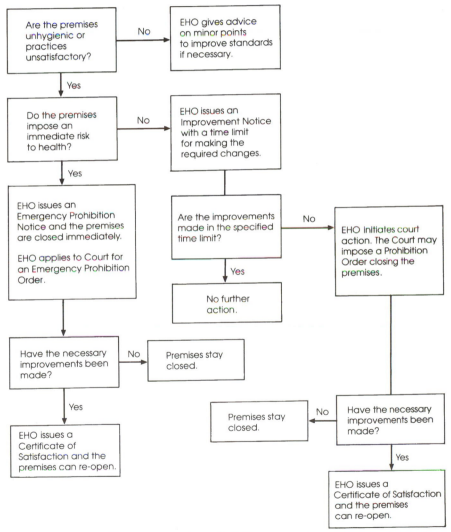

Actions open to an Environmental Health Officer when inspecting food premises

Penalties

Food hygiene offences are usually brought to a Magistrates' Court where the penalty for contravening the legislation is a maximum fine of £5000 for each offence and/or a prison sentence of up to six months. If the offence concerns false or misleading labelling or contamination (Food Safety Act, 1990) there is a maximum fine of £20 000. Food hygiene offences can be brought to a Crown Court. There is no maximum fine in a Crown Court and a prison sentence of up to two years may be imposed.

Chapter 11

Bacteria that Commonly Cause Food Poisoning

The names of the bacteria that cause the majority of outbreaks of food poisoning are:

- *Salmonella*
- *Campylobacter*
- *Clostridium perfringens*
- *Staphylococcus aureus*
- *Bacillus cereus.*

The table shows the causative agents in 1562 cases of bacterial food poisoning.

Food vehicle	Salmonella	Clostridium perfringens	Staphylococcus aureus	Bacillus cereus	Total
Chicken	51	19	2	3	75
Turkey	28	11	1	1	41
Poultry	3	1	–	–	4
Beef	5	21	4	1	31
Pork/ham	18	17	5	1	41
Lamb/mutton	1	3	–	–	4
Mixed and other meats, pies and sausages	36	35	3	6	80
Gravy/sauces	–	3	–	–	3
Milk/cream	13	–	–	–	13
Eggs	44	–	3	1	48
Pasta dishes	2	4	–	1	7
Rice	1	–	–	13	14
Shellfish/fish	6	1	2	1	10
Other mixed foods	18	12	10	27	67
Not known	1089	32	–	3	1124
Total	1315	159	30	58	1562

Source: Public Health Laboratory Service Communicable Disease Surveillance Centre

All bacteria have two names: a generic name and a specific name. The generic name is written first with a capital letter – for example, *Salmonella*, *Staphylococcus*. The specific name is written with a small letter after the generic name – for example, *aureus, perfringens, cereus*. There are approximately 2000 species of the *Salmonella* genus (for example, *Salmonella typhimurium*, *Salmonella enteritidis*), but since most of them cause food poisoning it is usual to talk about *Salmonella* food poisoning without distinguishing between them.

Identifying the type of food poisoning

It is normally possible to identify the bacteria that have caused a particular outbreak of food poisoning by laboratory examination of any remaining suspect food and the vomit or faeces of people suffering from the illness. However, it is often possible to be reasonably certain of the cause without laboratory tests by consideration of the suspect food, the incubation period, the duration of the illness and the symptoms:

- The **incubation period** is the time that passes between the entry of the poisonous food into the body and the occurrence of the first symptoms.
- The **duration** of the illness is the time between the appearance of the first symptoms and the recovery of the patient.
- The **symptoms** are usually predominantly vomiting or predominantly diarrhoea with or without fever, nausea and abdominal pains.

The way in which bacteria cause illness varies slightly: some bacteria (*Salmonella*, *Campylobacter*) cause infective food poisoning whereas others (*Staphylococcus aureus*, *Bacillus cereus*) cause toxic food poisoning.

Infective food poisoning

This type of food poisoning occurs when living bacteria are present in the food when it is eaten. Some of these bacteria are destroyed by the acid in the stomach but some survive. On reaching the neutral conditions of the small intestine, these bacteria start to multiply and irritate the lining, causing diarrhoea, nausea and abdominal pains. The incubation period is relatively long (usually 12 hours or more).

Toxic food poisoning

This type of food poisoning is caused by bacteria that produce a toxin while they are multiplying in food. When the food is eaten, the pre-formed toxin irritates the lining of the stomach, causing vomiting. If some of the toxin gets past the stomach to the small intestine, it may cause abdominal pains and diarrhoea. Living bacteria are not necessarily present in the food in this type of food poisoning. If the food has been heated before serving, the temperature reached may have been sufficient to destroy the bacteria but insufficient to destroy the toxin. Since the toxin is present in the food when it is eaten, the incubation period is relatively short (one to six hours).

Salmonella

Salmonella bacteria are small rod-shaped bacteria that cause infective food poisoning. The most common species in the UK are *Salmonella typhimurium* and *Salmonella enteritidis*.

Salmonella bacteria are commonly found in association with animals. Raw meat, eggs and the presence of pests are the main sources of *Salmonella* in the kitchen. Animal feed is frequently contaminated with *Salmonella* and this, together with intensive rearing methods, means that the majority of chickens and many other farm animals carry *Salmonella* in their intestines. The animals often do not show any signs of illness, but when they are slaughtered, bacteria from their intestines spread to the surface of the meat.

Salmonella bacteria are not very resistant to heat: they are destroyed in one or two minutes in boiling water. Thus, any food that has been thoroughly cooked and is served within a short time will not be a cause of *Salmonella* food poisoning. Most outbreaks are in fact caused by carelessness in food preparation. The most usual reason for *Salmonella* food poisoning is cross-contamination from raw meat to cooked food that is not heated again before being eaten. Another major cause of *Salmonella* food poisoning is inadequate thawing of poultry: this leads to undercooking in the centre of the bird, allowing *Salmonella* to survive, grow and multiply there.

Towards the end of 1988 and the beginning of 1989, the number of outbreaks of *Salmonella* food poisoning caused by hens' eggs increased dramatically. Previously, it had been thought that bacteria from infected hens did not get into the egg, but it now seems likely that bacteria can be present in the yolk of the egg before it is laid. The number of infected eggs is still thought to be very small but food handlers should be aware of the risk. Vulnerable groups, such as the sick, the elderly and young children, should never eat undercooked eggs. As it is not uncommon for the egg shell to be contaminated with *Salmonella*, care must be taken not to transfer bacteria from the shell to other foods. Bulk, liquid egg should only be purchased if it has been pasteurised, since it is an ideal medium for bacterial growth and one small piece of shell could contaminate a whole batch.

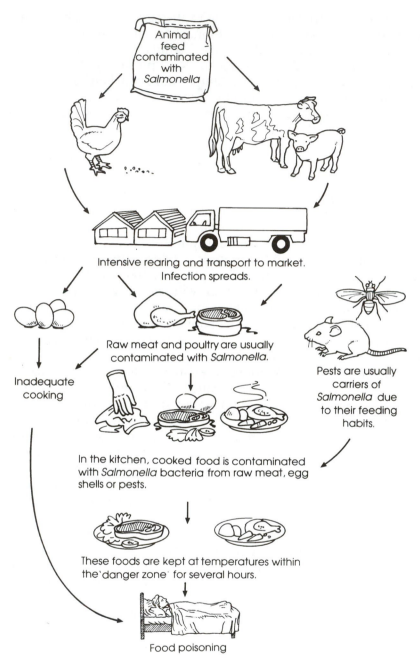

The causes of food poisoning by *Salmonella*

The risk of *Salmonella* food poisoning from eggs can be reduced if the following guidelines are observed:

- Hands should be washed after handling eggs.

- Eggs should be cooked thoroughly. Raw or lightly cooked eggs and uncooked foods made from them, e.g., mayonnaise, should be avoided, particularly by vulnerable groups. Pasteurised liquid egg and dried egg are available as safe alternatives to raw eggs.
- Cracked eggs should not be used.
- Eggs should be stored in a cool place, preferably the refrigerator.
- Ducks' eggs are more likely to be contaminated with *Salmonella* than hens' eggs, so thorough cooking of these is essential.

The incubation period for *Salmonella* food poisoning is usually 12–24 hours and the main symptoms are diarrhoea, abdominal pain, fever, headache and sometimes vomiting. Recovery usually takes anything from a day to one week, but the illness can be fatal in the elderly, the sick or the very young.

Campylobacter

Bacteria called *Campylobacter jejuni* and *Campylobacter coli* are the commonest cause of diarrhoea in the UK. *Campylobacter* infection is

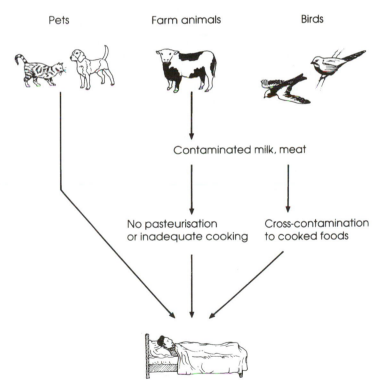

The causes of food poisoning by *Campylobacter*

similar in many ways to *Salmonella* infection: illness is caused by the presence of living bacteria in food when it is eaten. Unlike most types of food poisoning, however, the number of bacteria that must be present to cause illness is low, and food merely transports the bacteria without necessarily allowing their multiplication. As *Campylobacter* is not heat resistant, food that has been adequately cooked should not present any risk, as long as it has not been cross-contaminated after cooking.

Campylobacter, like *Salmonella*, is also associated with animals. It is possible that some human infections occur as a result of direct contact with farm animals, pets and birds. For this reason, it is essential to keep dogs, cats and other pets out of an industrial kitchen. They are also best kept out of a domestic kitchen; however, if this is not possible, they should not be allowed to walk over surfaces used for food preparation, or eat from bowls or plates that are used for human food. Bowls used for pets should be washed separately from the main wash. Any faeces, urine or vomit from pets should be cleared up immediately and the area disinfected.

Many cases of *Campylobacter* food poisoning have been caused by undercooked chicken and by foods that have been cross-contaminated by raw meat or poultry. Unpasteurised milk is also known to be a cause and several cases have been traced to pasteurised milk drunk from bottles where tops have been pecked by a bird on the doorstep.

In developing countries, many cases of *Campylobacter* infection are caused by contaminated water.

The incubation period for *Campylobacter* food poisoning is three to five days and the main symptoms are fever followed by severe diarrhoea and abdominal pain. Recovery takes from one to ten days.

Clostridium perfringens

Clostridium perfringens are rod-shaped bacteria that can form spores when conditions are unfavourable for growth.

Clostridium perfringens is frequently present in human and animal intestines, and in soil in the spore form. It therefore comes into the kitchen via raw meat, vegetables or a human carrier.

Clostridium perfringens does not produce a toxin while growing in food. However, when contaminated food is eaten, the bacteria revert back to the spore form and produce a toxin in the intestinal tract which causes illness between 8 and 22 hours after eating the food. This type of food poisoning is neither toxic food poisoning or infective food poisoning but has some characteristics of both.

Clostridium perfringens prefers to grow in the absence of oxygen, although it will tolerate a small amount. The majority of outbreaks are

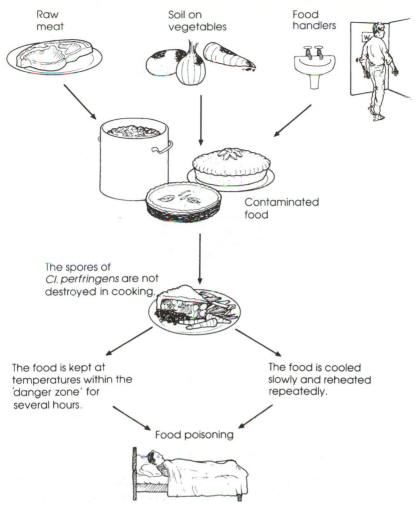

Raw meat

Soil on vegetables

Food handlers

Contaminated food

The spores of *Cl. perfringens* are not destroyed in cooking.

The food is kept at temperatures within the 'danger zone' for several hours.

The food is cooled slowly and reheated repeatedly.

Food poisoning

The causes of food poisoning by *Clostridium perfringens*

caused by meat and poultry dishes that have been pre-cooked, cooled slowly, allowing the multiplication of the bacteria, and then reheated inadequately before serving.

The main symptoms of *Clostridium perfringens* food poisoning are profuse diarrhoea, abdominal pain and nausea but rarely vomiting. Recovery usually occurs within 12 to 48 hours.

Staphylococcus aureus

Staphylococcus aureus are round bacteria that produce a toxin while growing and multiplying on food. If this food is then eaten, food

Humans carry *Staphylococcus* in their nose, mouth
and hair, on hands and in septic cuts, boils and styes.

Food handlers contaminate food which
requires little or no further cooking.

These foods are kept at temperatures
within the 'danger zone' for several hours.

Food poisoning

The causes of food poisoning by *Staphylococcus aureus*

poisoning can result. *Staphylococcus aureus* is not very resistant to heat
and is destroyed in one or two minutes in boiling water. However, the
toxin it produces is more heat resistant and can survive for approximately 30 minutes.

Staphylococcus aureus is frequently present in the nose, mouth and
on the skin of healthy people, and is present in large numbers in septic
cuts, boils and styes. Most outbreaks of *Staphylococcus* food poisoning
are caused by direct contamination of cooked food by food handlers
carrying the bacteria and subsequent storage of the food at warm temperatures, allowing the bacteria to multiply and produce toxin. Cold
meats and prepared sweets, such as gateaux and trifles, are frequently a
cause of this type of food poisoning.

The incubation period of *Staphylococcus* food poisoning is one to six
hours and the main symptom is sudden severe vomiting which is sometimes accompanied by abdominal pain and diarrhoea. Recovery usually occurs within 6 to 24 hours.

Bacillus cereus

Bacillus cereus are rod-shaped bacteria that produce a toxin while growing and multiplying on food. Food poisoning can occur if the contaminated food is eaten. They are able to form spores when conditions become unfavourable for growth.

Bacillus cereus is often present in the spore form in rice and other cereals, spices and cornflour. The majority of cases of *Bacillus cereus* food poisoning are caused by rice that has been pre-cooked, stored in warm conditions and then served cold or reheated. Toxin is produced by the bacteria during the storage period and is not destroyed by a quick reheating.

Bacillus cereus can cause two different types of food poisoning. One

Spores of *B. cereus* are present in dried rice, spices and cornflour.

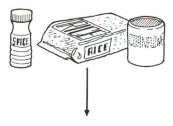

The spores are not destroyed in cooking.

The food is kept at temperatures within the 'danger zone' for several hours.

The food is cooled slowly and reheated repeatedly.

Food poisoning.

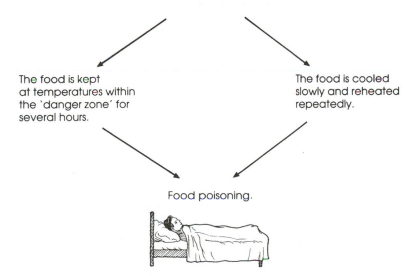

The causes of food poisoning by *Bacillus cereus*

type is very similar to *Staphylococcus* food poisoning, with a sudden onset of symptoms, mainly vomiting, between one and six hours after eating the food. The other type is similar to *Clostridium perfringens* food poisoning, in which the main symptom is diarrhoea and the incubation period is between 8 and 16 hours. In both instances, recovery occurs within 24 hours.

Listeria monocytogenes

Cases of illness attributed to *Listeria monocytogenes* are relatively rare but these bacteria have recently attracted a lot of attention partly because the illness it causes can be serious or even fatal, and partly because it is one of the few pathogenic bacteria that can grow at refrigeration temperatures.

Listeria monocytogenes is found widely distributed in the environment and is present in the intestines of many domestic and wild

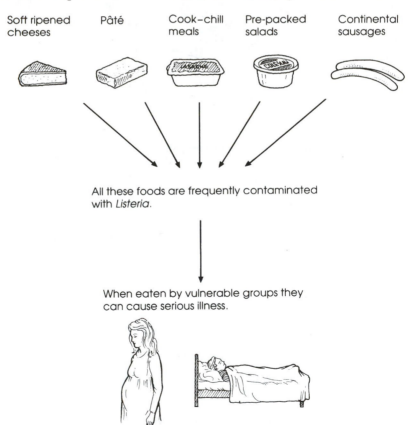

The causes of food poisoning by *Listeria monocytogenes*

animals, including chickens, sheep and cattle. The bacteria can be passed into the milk of infected animals.

The vast majority of people who eat food contaminated with *Listeria monocytogenes* will be unaffected, or, at worst, may have a mild fever for a short time. However, two groups of people are particularly at risk of severe illness: pregnant women and sick people whose illness or treatment affects their immune system. Listeriosis in pregnant women can cause miscarriage or result in a stillbirth. In very young babies and in immunosuppressed patients, listeriosis can give rise to meningitis and septicaemia.

Foods that have frequently been found to contain *Listeria*, and which should therefore be avoided by the two vulnerable groups, include soft ripened cheeses, for example, Brie and Camembert, pâté, cook–chill meals, coleslaw and other pre-packed salads in dressings, salami and continental sausages.

Cook–chill meals

Listeria monocytogenes only grows slowly at refrigeration temperatures but since recent research has shown that approximately 20% of cook–chill meals are infected, it is important to observe the storage instructions, the 'eat by' date on the packet and the heating instructions. *Listeria* does not form a spore, so thorough heating of the meal will ensure that it is safe to eat. Great care must be taken to ensure thorough and uniform heating if cook–chill meals are reheated in a microwave. The food must be cooked for the required length of time on the stated power setting and in the correct position. Instructions for standing times must also be observed because the food continues to cook by conduction during this period.

Summary of bacteria that commonly cause food poisoning

Bacteria	Access to food from:	Incubation period	Duration	Foods usually involved
Salmonella (infection)	Raw meat and poultry; eggs; pests and domestic pets; human carriers	6–72 hours (usually 12–24)	1–7 days	Cold meats and other dishes served cold that have been cross-contaminated after cooking; undercooked poultry
Campylobacter (infection)	Animals, pets, birds; raw meat	3–5 days	1–10 days	Undercooked poultry; unpasteurised milk; any food that has been cross-contaminated after cooking
Cl. perfringens (toxin in intestine)	Raw meat; soil on vegetables; human carriers	8–22 hours (usually 12–18)	12–48 hours	Meat casseroles, meat pies, minced meat dishes, reheated meat dishes
S. aureus (toxin in food)	Food handlers with septic cuts, boils or styes; sneezing and coughing over food	1–6 hours (usually 2–4)	6–24 hours	Cold meats and cream products that have been contaminated by food handlers during preparation
B. cereus (toxin in food)	Rice, cereals, cornflour, spices	1–16 hours	6–24 hours	Reheated rice dishes

Chapter 12
The Prevention of Food Poisoning

The total number of reported cases of food poisoning increases most years. This increase has been particularly rapid in the last few years, as shown in the table. The figures shown in the table only represent the number of reported cases, which are those where the sufferer has been sufficiently ill to consult a doctor. Since food poisoning often only lasts for a day or less, and most cases clear up without treatment, the majority of sufferers do not go to their doctor, and so these are not included in the official figures. If the sufferer does go to the doctor and the doctor suspects food poisoning, a sample of the sufferer's faeces or vomit is sent to the laboratory for examination. If tests confirm the presence of food poisoning bacteria, only then does the case become an official statistic. The actual number of cases of food poisoning is thought to be somewhere between 10 and 100 times the number of reported cases.

Reported cases of bacterial food poisoning 1985–94

Year	1985	1986	1987	1988	1989
No of cases	13 143	16 502	20 363	27 826	38 086

Year	1990	1991	1992	1993	1994
No of cases	36 945	35 291	42 551	44 271	50 692

Reported cases of illness attributed to *Campylobacter*

1988	1989	1990	1991	1992	1993	1994
28 761	32 526	34 552	32 636	38 552	39 385	44 317

Source: Public Health Laboratory Service Communicable Disease Surveillance Centre

Despite the relatively short duration of the illness, the sufferer can feel extremely unwell. In addition, because of the rapid onset, the sufferer is quite likely to be taken ill away from home, making it difficult to cope with sickness and diarrhoea. Food poisoning has, for many people, ruined a holiday, a wedding or other celebration, an important business meeting or a journey. In addition, many days of work are lost through people suffering from food poisoning, so the increasing number of cases is a cause for great concern.

Common faults in food preparation

A study of nearly 1500 outbreaks of food poisoning highlighted the 12 most common faults in food preparation.

Common faults in food preparation – the top 12

1. Food prepared too far in advance.
2. Food stored at room temperature.
3. Cooling food too slowly before refrigerating it.
4. Inadequate reheating of food.
5. The use of cooked food contaminated with food poisoning bacteria.
6. Undercooking meat and meat products (including poultry).
7. Incomplete thawing of frozen meat and poultry.
8. Cross-contamination from raw to cooked food.
9. Storing hot food below 63°C.
10. Infected food handlers.
11. Use of left-overs.
12. Extra large quantities of food prepared.

Food prepared too far in advance/food stored at room temperature

Nearly 60% of the incidents analysed identified the advance preparation of food as one of the factors causing the outbreak of food poisoning.

Most catering establishments have a busy period at lunch time and in the evening, making it necessary to prepare food in advance of requirements. This is a perfectly acceptable practice, provided that the temperature of the food is strictly controlled after preparation so that it is not left for any length of time in a warm environment. It must be either refrigerated or placed in hot-holding equipment pre-heated to 63°C or above.

High-risk foods must be kept at a temperature below 8°C or above 63°C unless they are to be consumed within two hours.

Cooling food too slowly before refrigerating it

Clostridium perfringens is likely to be present in foods prepared from raw meat or vegetables. It forms heat-resistant spores that survive most cooking procedures. For this reason, quick cooling of foods that are to be reheated at a later time is essential, so that there is insufficient time for the spores to germinate and for bacteria to multiply to large numbers.

> Food that is to be served cold or reheated must be refrigerated within $1\frac{1}{2}$ hours of cooking.

Inadequate reheating of food

Food that has to be reheated must be reheated thoroughly to ensure that the temperature at the centre of the food (especially large volumes) is high enough to destroy any food poisoning bacteria that are present. Reheating meat by adding a hot gravy or sauce to it and then keeping it warm before it is eaten has caused many outbreaks of food poisoning.

> Food that is reheated must reach an internal temperature of 70°C for at least two minutes.

The use of cooked food contaminated with bacteria

The number of catering premises that serve take-away meals is increasing, as is the number of outbreaks of food poisoning associated with this type of meal. Outbreaks involving cooked meats, cooked poultry and meat pies are also increasing. Sometimes the food is already poisonous at the time it is bought due to faults in the way it was prepared and stored before sale. Alternatively, it may have been contaminated during its preparation and storage at the wrong temperature by the purchaser allows bacterial multiplication to a level at which the food becomes poisonous.

Large-scale factory production of foods is normally very carefully controlled, but a slight error at some stage in production could lead to thousands of heavily contaminated or poisonous pre-cooked meals being distributed throughout the country. The cause of outbreaks occurring over a wide area is very difficult to trace.

> Great care must be taken not to contaminate foods that will not be cooked again after purchase.

Undercooking meat and meat products (including poultry)/incomplete thawing of frozen meat and poultry

Cooking from frozen is safe for small items where heat will penetrate rapidly, but large volumes of food must be thoroughly defrosted before cooking. The majority of chickens and turkeys are contaminated with *Salmonella*. Failing to defrost these before cooking leads to undercooking with the result that bacteria survive in the centre of the bird.

> Frozen meat and poultry must be thoroughly defrosted before cooking.

Cross-contamination from raw to cooked food

If contaminated raw food and cooked food are prepared on the same work surface or by using the same equipment, such as mincers, chopping boards and knives, cross-contamination will take place and the cooked food will be contaminated with food poisoning bacteria. Food handlers can also cause cross-contamination if they fail to wash their hands in between handling raw food and cooked food.

> Separate surfaces and equipment must be used for raw and cooked foods.

Storing hot food below 63°C

Hot cupboards and bains-marie can be used to keep food hot before it is served. If they are running at the correct temperature, they will keep the food above 63°C, which will prevent bacterial multiplication. Food poisoning outbreaks occur as a result of the incorrect use of hot-holding equipment, either because the equipment is not pre-heated before hot food is put in it or because it is used to reheat cold food.

Infected food handlers

Many of the food poisoning outbreaks involving *Staphylococcus aureus* are caused by food handlers contaminating high-risk food during its preparation. The most usual ways of contaminating the food are by sneezing over it or by failing to cover a septic cut on the hand.

Salmonella food poisoning outbreaks are sometimes caused by food handlers who are carriers of *Salmonella* and have failed to wash their hands after a visit to the toilet. Food handlers who suffer from *Salmonella* food poisoning must not handle food until they have been free of symptoms for 48 hours.

Use of left-overs

The use of food left over from meals served earlier in the day or on the previous day has caused a number of outbreaks. Left-over food should not be kept at room temperature while awaiting a decision about whether to use it at a later date. Any food that may be used again must be refrigerated immediately and then eaten cold or thoroughly reheated.

A modern, hygienic kitchen

Extra large quantities of food prepared

There is always a tendency to cater for extra large numbers on special occasions such as Christmas or a wedding reception. This is very unwise unless there is refrigeration space for *all* high-risk foods. Many large outbreaks of food poisoning have occurred at functions where the capacity of the catering establishment has been stretched too far. It takes many years for a catering establishment to recover its reputation if it is responsible for such an outbreak.

A strategy for the prevention of food poisoning

Food poisoning is easily prevented. There is general agreement that the best approach to reduce the numbers of food poisoning outbreaks is to ensure better education of food handlers and hence hygienic practices in all food premises.

An analysis of 592 food poisoning outbreaks showed that restaurants are responsible for the majority of outbreaks:

Place of outbreak	Number of outbreaks
Restaurant/reception/hotel	253
Hospital	80
Institution	61
School	17
Community	18
Shop	28
Canteen	27
Farm	5
Infected abroad	26
Other	22
Unspecified	55

To ensure that the catering establishment in which you work is not likely to cause an outbreak of food poisoning, check the following list. If the answer to any of these questions is 'no' or you are not sure, check the relevant chapter.

Prevention of food poisoning checklist

1. Are all the staff well trained in food hygiene and are regular training sessions held?
2. Do all staff maintain a high standard of personal hygiene? (See Chapter 4)
3. Are high-risk foods left on display at room temperature for longer than two hours? (See Chapter 2)
4. Are there adequate storage facilities for food including adequate refrigeration space? (See Chapter 6)
5. What arrangements are there for thawing frozen meat? (See Chapter 5)
6. What arrangements are there for quick cooling of food that is to be refrigerated? (See Chapter 5)
7. Is all food storage equipment working well and at the correct temperature? (See Chapter 6)
8. Is the kitchen well planned so that waste food and raw food do not come into contact with cooked food? (See Chapter 7)
9. Are the preparation areas spacious with separate areas for vegetables, raw meat and cooked foods? (See Chapter 7)
10. Is the washing-up process satisfactory? (See Chapter 8)
11. Is the kitchen and equipment cleaned on a regular basis? (See Chapter 8)
12. Are there any signs of a pest infestation? (See Chapter 9)
13. Is there an adequate number of toilet facilities and wash basins maintained to the standard required by law? (See Chapters 7 and 10)

If you have any doubts about the catering methods used or the standard of hygiene where you work, discuss the matter with your manager, who should contact an environmental health officer if further advice is needed.

Examination Questions

This book covers the syllabuses of:

- The Royal Institute of Public Health and Hygiene Primary Certificate in Food Hygiene.
- The Institution of Environmental Health Officers Basic Food Hygiene Certificate.
- The Royal Society of Health Essential Food Hygiene Certificate.

The examination set by The Royal Institute of Public Health and Hygiene (RIPHH) and that set by The Institution of Environmental Health Officers (IEHO) consists of 30 multiple-choice questions.

The examination set by The Royal Society of Health (RSH) consists of 20 multiple-choice questions.

Test yourself on the following questions.

Multiple-choice questions

1. Which of the following is the most common cause of food poisoning?
   (a) Red kidney beans
   (b) Moulds
   (c) Bacteria
   (d) Toadstools

2. Which one of the following statements best describes the effect that food poisoning bacteria usually have upon food?
   (a) It appears normal but it tastes horrible.
   (b) It appears stale and dry and it has an 'off' taste.
   (c) It tastes, smells and looks normal.
   (d) It appears and tastes normal but it has an unpleasant smell.
       (RSH)

3. Which one of the following statements is true?
   (a) All bacteria are harmful.
   (b) Some bacteria are harmful.
   (c) No bacteria are harmful.
   (d) Only bacterial spores are harmful.   (IEHO)

4. At which of the following temperatures will food poisoning bacteria multiply most rapidly?
   (a) 5°F
   (b) 37°C
   (c) 37°F
   (d) 63°C

5. Which one of the following pairs of people are at special risk from food poisoning?
   (a) Nurses and children
   (b) Children and old people
   (c) Old people and chefs
   (d) Chefs and nurses   (IEHO)

6. Which of the following is most likely to be a source of food poisoning bacteria?
   (a) Frozen peas
   (b) Pasteurised milk
   (c) Tinned salmon
   (d) Raw meat

7. Which one of the following food poisoning bacteria is transferred to food by coughing and sneezing?
   (a) *Bacillus cereus*
   (b) *Salmonella*
   (c) *Staphylococcus aureus*
   (d) *Clostridium perfringens*   (RSH)

8. When, by law, must you remember to wash your hands?
   (a) Before eating your lunch
   (b) Before smoking
   (c) Before handling high-risk foods
   (d) Before handling low-risk foods

9. The main reason for not allowing smoking in food preparation areas is because:
   (a) the fingers become contaminated with saliva
   (b) smoke causes cancer
   (c) it wastes time
   (d) ashtrays make the kitchen look untidy

10. What should you do if you cut yourself at work?
    (a) Grin and bear it.
    (b) Cover the wound with lint and a bandage.
    (c) Stop work and go home.
    (d) Cover the wound with a waterproof dressing.   (IEHO)

11. People who handle food should keep their fingernails:
    (a) smooth
    (b) short
    (c) varnished
    (d) long

12. The main reason why hair must be covered is that:
    (a) long hair gets in your eyes
    (b) hair and dandruff can fall into food
    (c) hats look smarter
    (d) hats keep your hair clean   (IEHO)

13. What is the maximum time you should leave food to cool before putting it into the fridge?
    (a) 20 minutes
    (b) $1\frac{1}{2}$ hours
    (c) 3 hours
    (d) 8 hours

14. Large pieces of meat should not be used because they take too long to:
    (a) prepare
    (b) brown
    (c) carve
    (d) cool   (IEHO)

15. If food is reheated, to what temperature and for how long should it be heated?
    (a) 70°C for 2 minutes
    (b) 50°C for 2 minutes
    (c) 50°C for 10 minutes
    (d) 30°C for one hour

16. Approximately how long does it take to defrost a 1.5 kg (3.3 lb) chicken in a refrigerator?
    (a) 20 minutes
    (b) 2 hours
    (c) 24 hours
    (d) 4 days

17. Which part of the refrigerator should be used for storing raw meat?
    (a) The door
    (b) The top shelf
    (c) The middle shelf
    (d) The bottom shelf

18. What is the correct operating temperature for a refrigerator?
    (a) 1°C–4°C
    (b) 8°C–63°C
    (c) –18°C
    (d) 100°C

19. At the temperature of a domestic refrigerator, most food poisoning bacteria:
    (a) die
    (b) multiply rapidly
    (c) form spores
    (d) are dormant

20. Which one of the following statements explains what is meant by the term 'Clean as you go'?
    (a) Clean down before you leave for home.
    (b) Clean up every hour throughout the day.
    (c) Once a year thoroughly clean the premises.
    (d) Clean up before moving on to the next task.   (RSH)

21. The main reason for keeping kitchens clean is:
    (a) to prevent contamination of food
    (b) to slow down bacterial growth
    (c) to reduce the chance of bacteria finding food
    (d) to give a good impression to customers

22. Which of the following methods of washing glasses will destroy bacteria?
    (a) Water at 20°C
    (b) Detergent and water at 20°C
    (c) Detergent and water at 50°C
    (d) Sanitiser and water at 50°C

23. Which one of the following steps will best prevent flies contaminating food?
    (a) Place food away from open windows.
    (b) Cover food with cling film.
    (c) Place food away from waste food bins.
    (d) Place food away from raw food.   (RSH)

24. Which of the following is a sign of a cockroach infestation?
    (a) Gnawed woodwork
    (b) An unpleasant smell
    (c) Fur and hairs
    (d) Torn packets of food

25. Which one of the following steps must be taken when mice are found in a food room?
    (a) Contact a pest control company.
    (b) Lay mouse bait.
    (c) Place mouse traps on the premises.
    (d) Ask the local chemist for advice.   (RSH)

26. Which one of the following could you be prosecuted for under the food laws?
    (a) Being late for work.
    (b) Combing your hair in the cloakroom.
    (c) Talking to your friends in a food room.
    (d) Smoking in a food room.

27. Which one of the following actions do the food laws require you to take should you have reason to believe that you are suffering from food poisoning?
    (a) Inform your employer of the problem.
    (b) Inform your workmates of the problem.
    (c) Continue work but wash your hands after handling raw meat.
    (d) Visit your doctor as soon as possible.

28. The food hygiene regulations state that food that is to be kept hot must be stored at a temperature above:
    (a) 5°C
    (b) 10°C
    (c) 37°C
    (d) 63°C

29. Which one of the following bacteria causes the greatest number of cases of food poisoning?
    (a) *Clostridium perfringens*
    (b) *Listeria*
    (c) *Staphylococcus aureus*
    (d) *Salmonella*

30. The main symptom of *Staphylococcus* food poisoning is:
    (a) vomiting
    (b) diarrhoea
    (c) fever
    (d) abdominal pains

Short-answer questions

1. What are the symptoms of food poisoning?

2. Name three causes of food poisoning apart from bacteria.

   (a)

   (b)

   (c)

3. (a) What are high-risk foods?

   (b) Name four high-risk foods.

4. Name three conditions which are necessary for bacterial growth.

   (a)

   (b)

   (c)

5. What is a bacterial spore?

6. What are the main sources of contamination in a kitchen?

7. What is meant by cross-contamination of food?

8. What is meant by 'colour coding' of kitchen equipment?

9. What sort of covering must be placed on an open cut?

10. List four occasions when food handlers should wash their hands.

   (a)
   (b)
   (c)
   (d)

11. Why should jewellery not be worn while working in the kitchen?

12. What is the main reason for not smoking while preparing food?

13. What is a thawing cabinet?

14. How would you prepare and store a beef casserole that is to be served the next day?

15. What does the four star symbol on a freezer indicate?

16. How would you keep food hot before it is served?

17. How should foods that will keep for more than three months be date marked?

18. What must a food handler do if he suffers from diahorrea or vomiting?

19. Describe how to deal with kitchen refuse.

20. Why is detergent necessary for washing dishes?

21. Why are wooden surfaces not recommended in food premises?

22. What is a disinfectant?

23. What should the manager of a food business do if there are any signs of a pest infestation?

24. Give three signs of an infestation by rodents.

    (a)

    (b)

    (c)

25. Who enforces food hygiene legislation?

26. What is the maximum fine that can be imposed in a Magistrate's Court for contravening the Food Safety (General Food Hygiene) Regulations 1995?

27. What is meant by the following terms in connection with food poisoning?
    (a) Incubation period:

(b) Infective food poisoning:

28. Name two bacteria that form spores.

29. Name two foods that are frequently contaminated with *Listeria* bacteria.

30. Name two groups of people who are at risk of severe illness from listeriosis.

Long-answer questions

Answer the following questions in approximately 50 words.

1. How can cross-contamination be prevented?

2. Describe the two-sink method of washing plates.

3. What is the risk of suffering from *Salmonella* food poisoning as a result of eating eggs?

4. What rules should be observed to maintain the correct temperature of a refrigerator?

5. Why should food not be refrozen once it has thawed?

Answers

Multiple-choice questions

1. c.	11. b.	21. a.
2. c.	12. b.	22. d.
3. b.	13. b.	23. b.
4. b.	14. d.	24. b.
5. b.	15. a.	25. a.
6. d.	16. c.	26. d.
7. c.	17. d.	27. a.
8. c.	18. a.	28. d.
9. a.	19. d.	29. d.
10. d.	20. d.	30. a.

Short-answer questions

1. Diarrhoea, abdominal pains, vomiting and nausea.
2. (a) Viruses; (b) Red kidney beans; (c) Chemicals.
3. (a) Foods that support bacterial growth and will be eaten without further cooking.
   (b) Cooked meat, boiled rice, cream, egg products.
4. (a) Food; (b) Moisture; (c) Warmth.
5. A protective casing that some bacteria can form when conditions are not suitable for their growth.
6. Raw meat and poultry, food handlers, animals, rodents, birds, insects, dust and refuse.
7. The transfer of bacteria from a contaminated source to an uncontaminated food.
8. A small coloured tag is fixed to the equipment to identify which equipment can be used for which type of food, e.g., equipment with a red tag can be used for raw meat but never for cooked meat.
9. A coloured waterproof plaster.
10. (a) After using the toilet; (b) After handling raw meat; (c) After smoking;
    (d) After handling refuse.
11. Because the skin underneath it remains moist and harbours bacteria, and there is a danger that small parts from the jewellery will fall into food.
12. People touch their lips when smoking and may transfer harmful bacteria on to their hands and so to food.

13. A special cabinet that maintains a constant temperature of 10°C–15°C and is used for thawing frozen food.
14. Cook it thoroughly, cool it rapidly and refrigerate it within 1½ hours of cooking. Reheat it thoroughly the next day and serve it immediately.
15. It indicates that the freezer is capable of freezing fresh food and that the operating temperature is –18°C.
16. Put it in a pre-heated hot cupboard or bain-marie and check that the temperature in the centre of the food is at least 63°C.
17. 'BEST BEFORE END' followed by the month and year.
18. Report the illness to his supervisor.
19. In plastic or steel bins with tight-fitting lids.
20. It removes grease.
21. Because wood absorbs water and is almost impossible to clean thoroughly.
22. A chemical that kills the majority of bacteria but does not destroy spores.
23. Contact a professional pest control company immediately.
24. (a) Droppings; (b) Gnawing marks; (c) Torn packets.
25. Each local authority through the work of environmental health officers and trading standards officers.
26. £5000 per offence.
27. (a) The time that passes between the entry of the poisonous food into the body and the occurrence of the first symptoms.
    (b) Food poisoning caused by living bacteria.
28. *Clostridium perfringens*, *Bacillus cereus*.
29. Soft cheeses, e.g., Brie and Camembert, cook–chill meals.
30. Pregnant women and sick people whose illness affects their immune system.

Long-answer questions

1. Cross-contamination between raw and cooked foods can be reduced by implementing a colour coding system in which a small coloured tag is fixed to equipment such as chopping boards and knives indicating that they may be used to prepare one type of food only, for example, raw meat or cooked meat. Cross-contamination can also be reduced significantly if food handlers wash their hands thoroughly after handling raw meat, vegetables coated with soil, eggs and refuse. Correct storage of foods in the refrigerator is also important. Cooked food should be covered and raw meat must always be stored below cooked food.

2. Firstly, food residues should be scraped from the plates. They should then be washed in the first sink containing hot water (50°C–60°C) and a detergent to remove any grease. The plates are then transferred to the second sink which contains water at 75°C–82°C. This will remove any traces of detergent and will also disinfect the plates, which can then be left to air dry.

3. If eggs are cooked thoroughly, there is no risk of them causing *Salmonella* food poisoning, but if they are eaten lightly cooked or raw as ingredients in mousse or mayonnaise there is a slight risk. These foods should not be eaten by vulnerable people such as young children, the elderly or the sick. Eggs should be stored in a refrigerator and used in rotation so they are always relatively fresh.

4. The correct running temperature of a refrigerator is between 1°C and 4°C. To maintain this temperature, the door should be kept shut whenever possible and food should be cooled to a temperature of 15°C before it is put in the refrigerator. It should be positioned in a well-ventilated area away from cooking appliances and out of direct sunlight, and should be defrosted regularly to prevent the build-up of ice around the refrigerating coils.

5. Bacteria are dormant in frozen food. When the food is thawed and the temperature of it reaches the danger zone, the dormant bacteria start to multiply. There will be more bacteria present when the food is frozen for a second time, all of which will multiply when the food is thawed again. If food is cooked after thawing, it may be refrozen once. There is also a noticeable loss in texture when food is thawed and refrozen.

Index

animals, as source of contamination 20–1, 87, 90
  see also pests

Bacillus cereus 17, 87, 93–4, 95
bacteria 3–4, 7, 10–17
  carriers of 19
  common causes of food poisoning 85–96
  effects of high and low temperatures on 15
  growth requirements 11–14
  number causing food poisoning 14
  reproduction 10–11
  spores 15–16
  toxins 16–17
  useful 4
  see also contamination
bactericidal soap 57–8, 66
berries, poisonous 8
binary fission 10–11
birds 20–1, 73, 76–8
blast freezers 47
bleach (hypochlorite) 65

Campylobacter 89–90, 95
canned foods 9, 41
  storage of 50–1
carriers of bacteria 19
ceilings, kitchen 57, 70
cheese 4
chemicals:
  cleaning agents 64–7
  pesticides 78
  poisonous 8–9
chillers 46
cleaning 63–72
  dishwashing 68–70
  of equipment 71
  hand-washing 25–6
  of kitchen 70
  materials for 64–7

  of microwave ovens 39
  process 67–71
  of refrigerators 45
  schedules 63–4
cling film 45
Clostridium perfringens 21, 40, 87, 90–1, 95, 99
clothing, of food handlers 26
cockroaches 73, 78
colour-coding, of equipment 23
contamination 18–24
  animals, rodents, birds, insects 20–1
  colour-coding equipment 23
  cross-contamination 22–3
  dust and refuse 21–2
  food handlers 19–20
  raw meat and poultry 18–19
Control of Pesticides Regulations (1986) 78
cook-chill meals 96
cooked food, contaminated 99–100
cooking food 32, 35–6, 100
cooling food 36–7, 99
covering food for storage 45
cross-contamination 22–3, 100
  refrigerators 34, 44–5
cuts, on handlers 19, 28–9, 101

danger zone, temperature 12, 32, 33
date marking of food 42
defrosting *see* thawing
design, of kitchens 53–5
detergents 64
dishwashing 64, 68–70
disinfection 65–6
display:
  freezers, open-top 47–8
  refrigerated cabinets 45–6
dry foods 13–14
  storage of 49–51
dust 21–2